Using Simulation
IN **Assessment**
AND **Teaching**

Using Simulation

IN **Assessment**
AND **Teaching**

Marion Bogo
Mary Rawlings
Ellen Katz
Carmen Logie

CSWE PRESS

Alexandria, Virginia

Library of Congress Cataloging-in-Publication Data

Bogo, Marion, author.
  Using simulation in assessment and teaching: OSCE adapted for social work / Marion Bogo, Mary Rawlings, Ellen Katz, Carmen Logie.
      pages cm
  Includes bibliographical references and index.
  ISBN 978-0-87293-171-8 (alk. paper)
  1. Social work education—United States. 2. Social workers—Training of—United States. 3. Simulated patients. I. Title.

  HV11.7.B64 2014
  361.3'2—dc23

                                                                    201402731

Printed in the United States of America on acid-free paper that meets the American National Standards Institute Z39-48 standard.

Council on Social Work Education
1701 Duke Street, Suite 200
Alexandria, VA 22314-3457
www.cswe.org

CONTENTS

ACKNOWLEDGMENTS

The development activities and research studies reported in this publication were supported by a grant from the Social Sciences and Humanities Research Council of Canada, the Royal Bank Fellowship Program, and the Building Professional Competence Research Initiative, Factor-Inwentash Faculty of Social Work, University of Toronto (http://research.socialwork .utoronto.ca/hubhomepage?hub=building_prof_competence).

Many colleagues contributed to the conceptualization, research studies, and implementation of the objective structured clinical examination (OSCE) adapted for social work at both the Factor-Inwentash Faculty of Social Work, University of Toronto, Ontario, Canada and Azusa Pacific University, California, United States of America. We wish to thank the following for their assistance through various phases of the many projects conducted to examine how simulation and the use of standardized clients could be used in teaching and in assessing educational outcomes. Both the Toronto and California project teams gratefully acknowledge the conceptual and methodological contributions of Dr. Glenn Regehr, co-investigator on the Toronto Social Sciences grant. The Toronto research team also benefitted from the involvement of Dr. Maria Mylopoulos, Dr. Lea Tufford, and Rachel Walliser. Thanks are extended to the many colleagues who joined us in developing scenarios and training standardized patients, including Dr. Nancy McNaughton and Kerrie Knickle of the Standardized Patient Program, Faculty of Medicine, University of Toronto; faculty colleagues Professor Andrea Litvack and Dr. Barbara Muskat; and experienced social workers in our field agencies. We truly appreciated the efforts of the many participants in the five-scenario OSCE research development project in 2008, social work students, recent graduates, and field instructors from the Factor-Inwentash Faculty of Social Work. We gratefully acknowledge the enthusiasm and commitment of Dean Faye Mishna of the Factor-Inwentash Faculty of Social Work who, once we had demonstrated the proof of concept in our original studies (Bogo, 2011a, 2011b; Bogo, 2013), provided resource support to implement and study an adapted OSCE for all students in the first year of the master's of social work program (Bogo, 2012). We greatly appreciate the collaboration of the many colleagues who have implemented the results of our studies on OSCE in a range of courses: Professor Andrea Litvack, director of the master's program, who facilitated the integration of the OSCE as the final assignment in an existing course; Eileen McKee, assistant dean, field education, who developed a procedure to use the OSCE to bridge course work and field practicum learning; and Barbara Lee, doctoral student, who provided invaluable assistance to Professors Michael Saini and Shelley Craig as they adopted teaching with simulation and worked toward developing an OSCE in courses on working with high-conflict families in child custody disputes and child protection and in social work practice in health settings, especially emergency rooms.

In 2012 Larry Enkin generously provided a private donation to the Factor-Inwentash Faculty of Social Work, Toronto, to support the integration of simulation into the master's program through innovative simulation-based teaching and a program of assessment. In 2014, based on the results of successful extension of the use of simulation in a variety of courses, Mr. Enkin provided further support to institutionalize the program. Such visionary commitment has ensured that we can continue to develop, study, and refine the use of simulation in social work education. The lessons learned from the ongoing program of development and research will be used as best practices in evidence-based teaching and assessment.

In California multiple people have contributed to the development and refinement of an OSCE program that has been used to assess student skills for the past 5 years. Thanks to Barbara Johnson, the lead instructor for the Practice I Skills course, who generously and enthusiastically embraced this method for the evaluation of students and the improvement of teaching. Erin Gaw, who has also supported this project since the beginning, thank you for your assistance in recruiting and training our amazing actors and actresses. The various faculty who have participated in rating students over the years; the students themselves, who gave their consent so that we could test our instrument and methods; and the actors and actresses must also be acknowledged. Without their participation and willingness we could not have done the work. And finally thanks go to Azusa Pacific University, which has supported this effort not only with teaching development grants but also by providing the autonomy and trust in the departments to allow the use of funds for teaching innovation and assessment.

Marion Bogo, *Toronto, Ontario, Canada*
Mary Rawlings, *Azusa, California, USA*
Ellen Katz, *Toronto, Ontario, Canada*
Carmen Logie, *Toronto, Ontario, Canada*

INTRODUCTION

The public expects professional education programs to ensure that graduating students have mastered the knowledge and skills necessary for ethical and effective practice. Assessing students' competence is essential to demonstrate that university programs accept their responsibility, are accountable for the education they provide, and can be trusted to prepare future generations of capable practitioners. Therefore, the accurate assessment of competence is of vital concern to all professional disciplines. As stated by the New Leadership Alliance for Student Learning and Accountability (2012):

> Those granting educational credentials must ensure that students have developed the requisite knowledge, skills, values, and attitudes that prepare them for work, life, and responsible citizenship. U.S. higher education must focus on both quantity and quality—increasing graduation rates and the learning represented in the degree. (p. 3)

Assessment of competence is a complex task, and educators and researchers in a range of professions have developed a substantial literature, including a range of approaches. Assessment entails articulating the components necessary for effective practice and developing assessment methods that are reliable and valid and can differentiate between students who possess the knowledge, skills, values, and judgment necessary for safe and effective practice and those who do not. In an era of increasing expectations that higher education institutions are accountable to the public, social work educators need reliable, valid, and authentic methods to assess educational outcomes and to demonstrate that they can be trusted with the responsibility of training, evaluating, and graduating new professionals.

Like health and human service professional education, social work education has shifted from a focus on curriculum structure and process to a focus on competency-based education. The former approach focuses on inputs and details the content and training experiences students must be exposed to for specified periods of time. The latter approach focuses on outcomes and articulates the complex set of behaviors reflecting knowledge, skills, values, and attitudes that students should be able to demonstrate on completion of the program. A competency-based approach has been adopted in many fields, including medicine (Carraccio, Wolfsthal, Englander, Ferentz, & Martin, 2002), psychology (Fouad et al., 2009; Kaslow et al., 2004), and nursing (Watson, Stimpson, Topping, & Porock, 2002).

In 2008 the Council on Social Work Education in the United States adopted a competency-based framework for the Educational Policy and Accreditation Standards (EPAS). This approach reflects a complex model of competence with its articulation of 10 key competencies and their related practice behaviors, which explicate each of the competencies. The competencies are as follows:

- Identify as a professional social worker and conduct oneself accordingly.
- Apply social work ethical principles to guide professional practice.
- Apply critical thinking to inform and communicate professional judgments.
- Engage diversity and difference in practice.
- Advance human rights and social and economic justice.
- Engage in research-informed practice and practice-informed research.
- Apply knowledge of human behavior and the social environment.
- Engage in policy practice to advance social and economic well-being and to deliver effective social work services.
- Respond to contexts that shape practice.
- Engage, assess, intervene, and evaluate with individuals, families, groups, organizations, and communities (CSWE, 2008).

As we are writing this text, drafts of the 2015 EPAS are being presented to the membership for feedback and consultation. The Office of Social Work Accreditation on behalf of the Commission on Educational Policy (COEP) and the Commission on Accreditation (COA) has noted, "since the 2008 EPAS reflected a significantly different approach focused on student competency, the commissions sought to simplify, clarify, and consolidate the existing educational policy and standards for Draft 1 of the 2015 EPAS" (CSWE, 2013, p. 1). As a result, we anticipate that the information in this text will remain useful to social work educators who, given the emphasis on competence and its assessment, are highly interested in developing a wide range of assessment methods to ensure that social work students are ready to graduate and take on professional roles. The competencies proposed for the 2015 EPAS (CSWE, 2014) are consistent with the 2008 version, but refinement has resulted in the following nine competencies, all expressed in action statements: Demonstrate ethical and professional behavior; engage diversity and difference in practice; advance human rights and social and economic justice; engage in practice-informed research and research-informed practice; engage in policy practice; engage with individuals, families, groups, organizations, and communities; assess individuals, families, groups, organizations, and communities; intervene with individuals, families, groups, organizations, and communities; and evaluate practice with individuals, families, groups, organizations, and communities.

Evaluation of social work students' learning is generally derived from assessments of their work in two domains: classroom courses and field practica. Classroom evaluation is based largely on assessing students' conceptual and written abilities in essays, tests, examinations, and journals (Crisp & Lister, 2002; Lister, Dutton, & Crisp, 2005). Before EPAS 2008, performance—the actual ability to use knowledge and skills in the service of clients and communities—was evaluated primarily and in most schools solely in the field practicum component of the curriculum. Field practicum evaluations are conducted by social work field instructors using a set of criteria provided by the social work academic program. The involvement of faculty field liaisons varies widely between programs (Bennett & Coe, 1998).

Elsewhere Bogo (2010, 2015) has noted that the most authentic evaluation of practice ability is observation and assessment of students while they are involved in actual practice. However, many concerns have been raised over time in the social work literature about the ability of field evaluations to identify differences in performance. Concerns include the lack of specificity in criteria used (Alperin, 1996; Kilpatrick, Turner, & Holland, 1994), the questionable reliability and validity of evaluation instruments (Bogo, Regehr, Hughes, Power, & Globerman, 2002; Gursansky & Le Sueur, 2011; Raskin, 1994; Regehr, Bogo, Regehr, & Power, 2007; Wodarski, Feit, & Green, 1995), inflation of ratings and a leniency bias (Sowbel, 2011; Vinton & Wilke, 2011), and the data used in assessing performance. For instance, studies have shown that many field instructors do not regularly observe students but instead rely on students' written and verbal reports of their practice (Maidment, 2000; Rogers & McDonald, 1995) and students' reflections in field supervision (Bogo & Vayda, 1998). A several-year program of research found that field instructors had extremely high agreement when evaluating performance of students they did not know (Bogo, Regehr, et al., 2004). However, they had great difficulty evaluating their own students for a range of reasons connected to the properties of rating scales (Regehr et al., 2007) and to the interpersonal dynamics in the student–field instructor relationship. Field instructors reported feeling very conflicted when pulled between providing critical feedback or failing grades and providing teaching based on social work values of prizing a nonjudgmental attitude and using strengths and empowerment approaches (Bogo, Regehr, Power, & Regehr, 2007). Similar findings were reported by Finch and Taylor (2013) in a study of practice teachers in England, where the term *practice teachers* refers to field instructors. (It is interesting to note these findings even though social work education is guided by a competence framework and, more recently in England, a capability framework.)

The findings of these studies can inform our approaches to orientation and training for field instructors in their evaluation role and in the design of new field evaluation instruments (see Regehr, Bogo, & Regehr, 2011, for an example of an innovative evaluation approach). However, of great importance is the uniform finding of grade inflation in evaluation of student practice. It appears that the intense field instructor–student relationship renders it extremely difficult for individual field instructors to provide evaluations that are standardized across settings and instructors. As a result, social work programs must take on greater responsibility for directly assessing student practice competence, moving beyond the primary reliance on field evaluations. The proposed EPAS captures the implications of the preceding discussion about assessment of competence in the following statement: "Assessment is best done while students are engaged in activities that approximate authentic practice tasks as closely as possible" (CSWE, 2014, p. 22). Our interpretation of this statement is that the policy recognizes the reality that assessment of competence will probably occur in field settings, but assessment should also occur through the use of other methods. Such methods must be close to practice, however. This emphasis in social work accreditation on assessment of competence can stimulate creative and innovative design and testing of new methods. New knowledge derived from such initiatives will ultimately contribute to a better understanding of components of professional competence and related effective assessment methods. We believe the objective structured clinical examination (OSCE) adapted for social work provides one such approach.

OSCE Adapted for Social Work

Initially working independently, the Toronto team and the California researcher became interested in examining the possibility of collaboration in using an OSCE for social work. We met informally in Toronto in 2005 with social work colleagues who were already interested in OSCE for social work: Professor Emeritus Wallace Gingerich, Case Western Reserve (Gingerich, Kaye, & Bailey, 1999), and Professor Eva Lu, New York University (Lu et al., 2011). We observed an OSCE at the University of Toronto Faculty of Medicine, conducted with medical students completing a rotation in psychiatry, and discussed the possibilities of using an OSCE in social work. A subsequent meeting at Case Western Reserve in Cleveland allowed the group to further explore the approach.

The aim at this stage was to examine whether a standardized, reliable, and valid assessment method could be used as a formal examination of student competence at various points in a program, such as at the completion of a course, at the end of an academic year, or at the end of an entire program. The expectation was that this examination would be part of a suite of assessment tools, noting that it could provide rich data integrating student learning from both courses and field practica. Other potential uses could include determining practice competence of BSW graduates who are entering a master's program with advanced standing; assessing competence at the end of specific specializations in the second year of a master's program; or, in schools that allow a challenge examination for exemption from part of the practicum, determining whether practice equivalence has been achieved.

This publication results from the experience of our two teams working separately and collaboratively. The Toronto Team consisted of educators, researchers, and doctoral students who developed, tested, and implemented this new approach to assessment of student competence. We used the model in a large graduate social work program, supported by research grants from the Canadian Social Sciences and Humanities Research Council, small institutional grants, and a generous gift from a private donor to institutionalize the program. Professor Mary Rawlings at the Azusa Pacific University, using institutional grants, developed and studied the use of an OSCE in an undergraduate program.

The two groups have developed an informal and highly productive partnership. Cases are shared, scales are used and modified, and lessons learned from each team inform the work of the other. In an effort to develop a community of social work educators and researchers interested in using simulation in teaching and standardized clients in assessment of student learning, both teams present their research findings at the Annual Program Meeting of the CSWE and jointly offer an annual Faculty Development Institute since 2009, provide workshops at the Association of Baccalaureate Social Work Deans and Directors conference, and since 2013 have organized a roundtable for educators to share experiences and materials. This publication is an attempt to respond to the interest and needs of attendees at the institute and other presentations who want to replicate the simulation and OSCE method in their own programs. The publication includes conceptual frameworks, detailed information about the method, and materials that can be used or modified.

In a systematic review of studies in social work education where standardized or simulated clients were used, we found that each study was unique, resulting in a lack of conceptual and empirical development of a knowledge base in this area (Logie et al., 2013). Variation was found in the content of case studies and outcome measures. In the interests of advancing social work education research and scholarship, this publication includes a number of well-described case scenarios for simulation and performance rating scales. It is our hope that a community of social work educators and researchers can collaborate in building an evidence base for the use of simulation in teaching and assessing student learning in social work.

Chapter 1 provides important frameworks for conceptualizing competence and understanding the implications for assessment using an OSCE adapted for social work. Chapter 2 provides guidance for designing an OSCE, including developing authentic scenarios and rating scales. Chapter 3 provides information for planning logistics, implementing the examination, and identifying resource needs. Chapter 4 discusses using simulation in teaching and student skill development, and for some educators it may be a good place to start, building toward using an OSCE for assessment of learning and competence. Chapter 5 introduces strategies for developing support and building an assessment program using OSCE, including university, administrative, faculty, and student support. This chapter also includes answers to questions that are frequently asked by participants at our presentations on the OSCE method. Throughout the publication, findings from our empirical studies on the OSCE are integrated into discussion of best practices and remaining challenges. The appendices provide a range of materials for use in an OSCE, such as a glossary of terms (Appendix A), rating scales (Appendix B), client scenarios (Appendix C), course material with sample assignments (Appendix D), forms for conducting an OSCE (Appendix E), and an example of the use of a video recording of simulated practice for teaching (Appendix F). Finally, two video recordings demonstrating the phases in the OSCE have been developed as an accompaniment to the text and can be accessed at http://youtu.be/vFSd9D6PF18 and http://youtu.be/JMvsgNVBrtk.

CHAPTER 1

Conceptualizing Competence and Implications for Assessment

Simulation can be used in a variety of ways to teach social work practice and to assess student learning. In related health professions education, simulation is considered a technique "to replace or amplify real experiences with guided experiences, often immersive in nature, that evoke or replicate substantial aspects of the real world in a fully safe, instructive, and interactive fashion" (Gaba, 2007, p. 126). Simulation environments range from the use of mannequins, devices, or software programs to human portrayal with standardized client actors. Pilots are trained using simulators, and this approach is effective in improving safety in situations with high risk and complexity.

Simulation with actors or colleagues is generally called human simulation, distinct from simulation with mannequins, games, or other devices. In this text the term *simulation* refers broadly to situations where students interact with other people, typically actors who are trained to portray clients in a practice setting in a fairly consistent manner. Simulations are also used in role play where students interact with peers or with the instructor, who is playing the client. Such simulations are used primarily in teaching. In contrast are simulations where actors portray clients in a practice situation in a consistent and standardized manner for the purpose of assessment, as in an objective structured clinical examination (OSCE). Because OSCEs involve rating students' performance and providing a grade (or pass/fail designation), it is important that actors' portrayal is standardized and consistent for each student. In these examinations student–actor interactions are observed by an assessor (instructor, trainer, or researcher), who may provide feedback at the time and generally uses rating scales to measure competence (Bogo, Regehr, Logie, et al., 2011). Although human simulation such as role play has been used in social work classrooms as a teaching tool for many years, using human simulation with standardized clients for assessment of student practice competence is more recent in social work. This text seeks to advance the use of simulation in teaching in social work and the use of simulation with standardized clients and scenarios in assessing social work students' competence. The text offers a conceptual framework informed by theory and research, with practical steps necessary to develop sound methods. In this way social work educators and researchers will build the reliability and validity needed for the effective use of simulation in educating students and assessing their competence.

A multiproject program of research on assessment of student performance has led to a conceptualization of competence that has informed our use of simulation and standardization, producing an educational and assessment process that is based on a theoretical and empirical foundation. Simulation can be used without such underpinnings. However, our team has found that our assessment and teaching efforts are enriched by a systematic approach that is guided by a competence framework to conceptualize educational goals and student outcomes. In an iterative fashion, through attempts to design authentic, reliable, and valid assessment procedures using simulation and standardization, our understanding of competence has evolved and deepened. This chapter begins with a discussion of concepts relating to competence, including models discussed in the literature and ideas developed from our studies, to provide a theoretical context for designing simulation experiences.

Competence in Social Work and Related Fields

The essence of competence is a focus on what practitioners or students are able to do in practice, rather than what they know. Professions identify a set of interrelated competencies that, when taken as a whole, reflect an integrated view of the ways in which practitioners perform as they carry out their roles in the domains associated with their profession. Typically, definitions of competence tend to include a set of knowledge, skills, and attitudes or values that are evident in professionals' behavior (Bogo, 2010; Cheetham & Chivers, 2005;

Hodges & Lingard, 2012; Kane, 1992). Competencies are broadly defined and conceptualized and then examined to identify their related parts. These parts may need further specification, especially when used to guide assessment. This view is similar to that of the Educational Policy and Accreditation Standards (EPAS) of the Council on Social Work Education (CSWE, 2008) when the first competency framework was introduced. In an explanatory document, Holloway, Black, Hoffman, and Pierce (2009) discuss competence as follows:

EPAS defines competencies as "measurable practice behaviors that are comprised of knowledge, values and skills" (Educational Policy [EP] 2.1). American Heritage adds the notion of "ability" to the definition. This suggests that the components of a competency share a commonality at least insofar as they all contribute to the ability in question. EPAS describes each of its competencies in a couple of sentences and then goes on to suggest the practice behaviors which constitute its elemental parts. Together these practice behaviors serve to operationalize the competency as well as to inform content utilized in curriculum design. Again, the competency is operationalized by the practice behaviors and evidence of student acquisition of the competency is demonstrated by the performance of the practice behaviors. Thus it is the demonstrated ability to execute an interrelated and comprehensive set of practice behaviors which EPAS takes as evidence of having acquired competency. (p. 2)

The concept of competence has a long history in social work education. In the mid-1970s social work educators in the United States proposed competency-based education as a unifying framework to integrate knowledge-based classroom learning and performance-based field learning. Educators (Arkava & Brennan, 1976; Clark & Arkava, 1979; Gross, 1981) identified a range of competencies, articulated specific behaviors with indicators that reflected increasing levels of performance, and urged the creation of reliable and valid evaluation methods of students' learning. Undergraduate programs embraced the approach, with some offering entire competency-based programs (Baer & Frederico, 1978). Some graduate programs also adopted competency frameworks, but these frameworks were applied mainly in the field practicum (Boitel, 2002). University-based courses continued to be designed in typical ways, focusing on content mastery as opposed to demonstrated practice competence.

As educators undertook projects to prepare social workers for specialized practice in particular fields, they used the concept of competence to develop competency frameworks. For example, the California Social Work Education Center (CalSWEC), a consortium of 12 schools of social work with graduate programs and 58 county-level public social service departments, defined competence as "properly or well qualified; capable; adequate for the purposes defined" (Berube, 1985, as quoted in Clark, 2003, p. 139) and "further implies expertise, proficiency, and mastery of a particular skill or body of knowledge" (Clark, 2003, p. 140). Over 20 years this consortium originally identified six competencies (multicultural and ethnic sensitive practice; core child welfare skills; social work skills and methods; human development and behavior; workplace management; and child welfare administration, planning, and evaluation), with further description of elemental skills for each including use of empirical literature and critical thinking. These original competencies have been realigned with the EPAS framework and describe advanced competencies and practice behavior indicators for specialized practice in public child welfare.

The Hartford Foundation-sponsored project for specialized practice in social work with older adults (Damron Rodriguez, 2008) used the work of Carraccio and colleagues (2002), who define competence as "being able to demonstrate that the knowledge, values, and skills learned can be integrated into practice" (2008, p. 27). Through iterative work drawing on the literature and focus groups of practitioners, four domains were identified (values, ethics, and theoretical perspectives; assessment; intervention; and aging services, programs, and policies), with 10 dimensions of competence expressed as skill subsets. These competencies have since been realigned with the EPAS framework.

Scholars in education and medicine worldwide, and in social work in the United Kingdom and Australia, were early adopters of competency-based models and have used them for many decades to understand and define the various aspects of knowledge, values, and skills needed to practice in the respective professions. A critique of these earlier models identified the tendency to deconstruct professional practice into ever-growing lists of discrete, specific behavioral skills (Hackett, 2001; Kelly & Horder, 2001). For example, medical educators caution against "the threat of reductionism ... breaking down competencies into the smallest observable units of behavior, creating endless nested lists of abilities that frustrate learners and teachers alike" (Frank, Snell, et al., 2010, p. 643). Others argue that the competence approach does not convey the organic nature of practice, in which skills are integrated and used in an interconnected manner.

In a move to improve the quality of social work services and education in England, the government established the Social Work Reform Board and adopted the recommendation of establishing "a set of overarching professional standards which will shape what social workers should know and do as students, as newly qualified social workers, and at different stages in their careers" (SWRB, 2010, p. 5). It appears that in an attempt to distance from a mechanistic view of competence, as discussed earlier, and a tick box approach, the standards are expressed as capabilities in a professional capability framework (College of Social Work [CSW], 2012a, p. 1). Taylor and Bogo (2013) provide a critical analysis of literature on terminology associated with professional competence in general and in specific professions such as social work and medicine. Of interest is the result of a systematic review of competency-based medical education conducted by an international team of researchers who conclude that the defining features of competence are that it refers to "multiple domains of ability ... multi-dimensional, dynamic, contextual, and developmental ... an ever-changing, contextual construct" (Frank, Snell, et al., 2010, p. 641). Taylor and Bogo (2013) conclude that although the terms *competence* and *capability* are used in a variable way in the literature, contemporary definitions are moving away from a reliance solely on observable measurable skills to include the crucial dimensions of professional practice that involve cognitive processing and professional judgment.

Conceptualizing Holistic Competence

Interested in developing a grounded understanding of competence, we conducted a multiproject program of research and elicited the practice wisdom of field instructors in both micro (Bogo et al., 2006) and macro practice (Regehr et al., 2012); specifically the implicit and explicit constructs they used when evaluating student performance. From our studies a complex view of competence emerged consisting of two interrelated dimensions (Bogo, 2010). As described in Bogo and colleagues (2013),

> one dimension, *meta-competence*, refers to higher order, overarching qualities and abilities of a conceptual, interpersonal, and personal/professional nature. This includes students' cognitive, critical, and self-reflective capacities. The second dimension, *procedural competence*, refers to performance and the ability to use procedures in various stages of the helping process and includes the ability for example, in direct practice, to form a collaborative relationship, to carry out an assessment, and to implement interventions with clients and systems. (p. 261)

In macro practice, procedural competence includes the ability to manage projects and to implement steps to achieve project goals (Regehr et al., 2012). Metacompetencies and procedural competencies are linked because the former guides the use of the latter, observable behavioral skills. As noted earlier, in social work, assessment of competence has emphasized procedural competence, representing a traditional or functional model of competence. However, as we interpreted findings from the aforementioned studies it became clear that when experienced social workers discussed competence, they highlighted the importance of dimensions such as critical thinking, self-awareness, and self-regulation. It became apparent that such dimensions affect the way a social worker engages in intentional and purposeful use of discrete behaviors and techniques, ideally leading to focused, integrated, and professional practice. This view of competence, one that considers both metacompetence and procedural competence, was seen as multidimensional and integrative and reflective of social work practice. We have conceptualized this view as holistic competence. A review of earlier and recent literature found this perspective compatible with those offered by scholars in related human services and health professions.

Scholars have discussed a holistic view of competence and referred to the importance of metacompetence. For example, the term *metacompetence* is used in related fields of management (Fleming, 1991; Hall, 1986), medicine (Harden, Crosby, Davis, & Friedman, 1999; Talbot, 2004), and professional psychology (Weinert, 2001) and refers to mental agility and creativity (Reynolds & Snell, 1988); problem-solving and analytic capacities (Cheetham & Chivers, 1996, 1998); and interpersonal communication, self-awareness, and self-development (Hatcher & Lassiter, 2007; Talbot, 2004). Harden and colleagues (Harden et al., 1999) propose that metacompetencies such as the ability to integrate theory, ethics, and emotional intelligence into clinical reasoning and judgment operate through the performance of basic competencies. Weinert (2001) suggests that the development of metacompetencies depends on self-awareness, self-reflection, and self-assessment. As emphasized earlier, these dimensions are critical in professional social work as well. Competent practitioners must be able to engage in such processes as critical thinking and self-reflection during and after the performance of professional practice.

An analysis of conceptions of competence in health professions education literature, and particularly in medical education, revealed that although definitions vary there is agreement that competence is composed of knowledge, skills, and "other components" (Fernandez et al., 2012, p. 357). Of interest in this discussion is the inclusion of the term *ability* as a frequently mentioned component. The authors note that "ability is generally composed of abstract reasoning, memory and the cognitive processes associated with solving novel questions" (p. 360). They consider these elements of competence as related to "clinical reasoning, professional socialization, communication and reflection in daily practice" (p. 360). This view is consistent with literature reviewed earlier and supports a broad and holistic view of competence.

From our studies we became interested in the way in which cognitive and subjective processes are apparent in notions of competence (Bogo et al., 2013; Katz, Tufford, Bogo, & Regehr, 2014). In medical education literature Epstein and Hundert (2002) noted the importance of considering the way in which the practitioner's use of knowledge and ways of thinking or habits of mind operate in framing, understanding, and assessing situations. These internal cognitive constructions of issues, strengths, and challenges in clients and communities reflect how practice is conceptualized, how knowledge is used, and how information is processed and affects judgments and decisions that guide intervention (Cheetham & Chivers, 2005; Eraut, 1994; Schon, 1983). The concept of tacit knowledge is useful in this regard because it highlights that professionals also draw on ideas, opinions, convictions, and assumptions they hold as a result of their personal and professional lived experiences. This knowledge may operate at an unconscious level, affecting decision making (Munro, 2011), and can be elicited through guided reflection (Bogo et al., 2013).

Integral to any discussion of professional judgment is the use of self by the practitioner. This perspective recognizes the crucial nature of the self in professional practice and the need for pedagogy to socialize students to think and perform like social workers (Larrison & Korr, 2013). Part of this enduring concept is the importance of social workers' emotional self-awareness, subjective understanding, and capacity to be self-reflective (Fox, 2011; Ruch, 2007). Recent contributions from neuroscience research highlight that practitioners' emotions and cognitions are linked. Our perceptions, appraisals, and decisions are significantly affected by the emotional context of practice (Immordino-Yang & Damasio, 2007; Kahneman, 2011). Munro (2011) points out the importance of understanding intuitive thinking and emotional responses in social work practice in child welfare. Drawing on neuropsychology research, Munro sees intuition as largely unconscious, rapid, and automatic. Our emotional responses to information and the experience we have when interacting with clients significantly affect our judgments. In turn these emotional responses are related to our tacit knowledge: what we have learned through our personal and professional experiences, the truths that are internalized and that are not easily explicitly identified. Therefore, holistic competence must include the ability to be self-aware of our subjective thinking, feeling, and reactions, especially with regard to the judgments we make. Accordingly, self-awareness and emotional self-regulation when involved in professional practice are important dimensions of holistic competence. Reflection may be a useful process by which to access these internal states and thoughts, to explicitly identify and critically examine the data in practice situations and interactions to which we are reacting. Cognitive processes and emotional states affect one's ability to carry out professional practice and therefore are incorporated in a holistic competence model (Bogo et al., 2013).

Finally, any discussion of competence includes the skills and techniques seen when one is observing practice. Skills operate in the service of enacting complex practice behaviors. For example, the competence of assessment will be enacted as a social worker collects information from a teenage client about suspected sexual abuse in the family and skillfully uses a range of communication and interviewing skills. Skills are used to enact practice behaviors, which in turn are demonstrations of competence. Other examples of complex practice behaviors in micro practice are building and maintaining collaborative relationships, conducting assessments, and providing interventions (Bogo, 2010; Bogo et al., 2006). In macro practice, complex practice behaviors identified in studies include developing collaborative relationships, providing leadership through project management, and the ability to articulate and implement steps to attain goals (Regehr et al., 2012).

Based on our studies noted previously and insights gained from scholars writing about competence in related fields, the conceptualization of holistic competence in social work shown in Figure 1 has evolved.

Figure 1. A model of holistic competence in social work.

To summarize, at the heart of any view of competence is the recognition that practitioners are engaged in carrying out complex practices and practice behaviors. A range of skills is used by social workers, including interviewing and interpersonal communication skills. However, the enactment of these practices is a product of the integration of many components. Figure 1 illustrates this perspective: Social workers use knowledge and skills guided by the way in which they engage in critical thinking to understand the situations they confront. They draw on theoretical and empirical knowledge as well as tacit knowledge derived from their lived experiences, both personal and professional. In contrast to earlier notions that viewed thinking and feeling as separate entities, contemporary neuroscientists have pointed out that affective, emotional, subjective reactions are integral to cognitive processes (Immordino-Yang & Damasio, 2007; Kahneman, 2011). Thus, professional judgment is based on the links between a practitioner's thoughts and feelings and the reflective and critical thinking she or he brings to the judgments and decisions made. Therefore, competence involves awareness of our emotional states, feelings, and reactions and the use of reflection and self-regulation to understand, manage, and work productively in practice. It appears that these latter dimensions are similar to the elements in the long-standing social work concept of use of self. Context is always significant in social work practice. So, too, in views of competence, practitioners are affected by the contexts in which practice occurs, such as the professional context, which provides values, standards, and a code of ethics; the organizational context, which provides a mandate, focus, and policy guidelines; and the community context, which includes factors unique to a particular geographic location or cultural or population group.

Furthering the notion of competence as expressed in EPAS 2008, the proposed EPAS 2015 (CSWE, 2014) identifies a holistic view of competence as follows:

> Competency-based education rests upon a shared view of the nature of competence in professional practice. Social work competence is the ability to perform complex practice behaviors in the delivery of professional service to promote human and community well-being. EPAS recognizes a holistic view of competence; that is, performance of practice behaviors is guided by knowledge, values, skills, and cognitive and subjective processes that include the social worker's critical thinking, subjective reactions, and exercise of judgment in regard to unique practice situations. Overall professional

competence is multidimensional and composed of interrelated competencies. An individual social worker's competence is seen as developmental and dynamic, changing over time in relation to continuous learning. (p. 2)

With respect to assessment of competence, the same view is evident. EPAS 2015 (CSWE, 2014) rests on a view of competence as holistic and multidimensional. Assessment must "capture the performance of the competencies and the quality of internal processing underlying the performance of the competencies while engaged in authentic practice tasks" (CSWE, 2014, p. 22).

As a final comment supporting the adoption of a broad definition of holistic competence, it is interesting that a similar perspective was adopted by social workers in England at approximately the same time as CSWE adopted a competence framework. Initially, through a highly consultative process, the Social Work Reform Board recommended the establishment of the College of Social Work. This body was established in 2012 and describes itself as

the centre of excellence for social work, upholding and strengthening professional standards to the benefit of the public. The College is an independent not for profit membership organisation, providing practical tools and resources to its members to enable them to uphold and strengthen standards of professional practice. (CSW, 2014)

Early in its inception, a professional capabilities framework was developed that defines the capabilities (as noted earlier, similar to the conceptualization of competence) that professional social workers are expected to attain and demonstrate throughout their professional careers. These capabilities are professionalism; values and ethics; diversity; rights, justice, and economic well-being; knowledge; critical reflection and analysis; intervention and skills; contexts and organizations; and professional leadership. The view that capabilities are integrated is expressed as follows:

The nine capabilities should be seen as interdependent, not separate. As they interact in professional practice, so there are overlaps between the capabilities within the domains, and many issues will be relevant to more than one domain. Understanding of what a social worker does will only be complete by taking into account all nine capabilities. (CSW, 2012b)

This view of competence is linked to holistic assessment efforts with the expectation that practice must be assessed in a holistic manner when evidence is presented that demonstrates the integration of learning across the nine domains.

A multidimensional conceptualization of holistic competence leads to the need for holistic assessment methods. The OSCE adapted for social work has been designed to assess interrelated components of competence and thus is ideal as one of a suite of assessment approaches that can be useful to promote student learning, assess competence, and provide important data to programs to inform curriculum design and ongoing efforts to improve learning and performance outcomes of graduates.

Assessing Competence: OSCE Adapted for Social Work

Educational or learning outcome assessment has been a topic of interest in higher education for the past 30 years. It appears that this literature uses various terms, sometimes interchangeably and sometimes defined somewhat differently. This can create confusion for social work educators as we approach the task of determining the effects of education on student learning and performance. Of interest for this discussion is the meaning of the term *assessment,* especially as used in the EPAS. Also, we are aware that the term *evaluation* has been used traditionally in social work, especially in regard to field practicum learning and student performance.

After reviewing the literature in higher education, in this text we use these two terms in the following way. *Assessment* is the act of measuring student learning and involves gathering credible evidence of inputs, such as educational activities, and outcomes, such as student performance, for the purpose of improving effectiveness of instruction and programs and of demonstrating accountability (Banta, 2013). The definition of assessment provided by Suskie (2009) is frequently used. She comments, "Assessment is the ongoing process of establishing clear, measurable expected outcomes of student learning, ensuring that students have sufficient opportunities to achieve those outcomes, systematically gathering, analyzing, and interpreting evidence to determine how well students' learning matches the expectations and using the resulting information to understand and improve student learning" (p. 4). The National Academy for Academic Leadership (2013) offers a similar definition and adds that information gathered can help make "effectual decisions about student learning and development, professional effectiveness, and program quality."

There are two types of assessment: Formative assessment is carried out during a course or program to provide feedback that students can use to improve learning and performance, and summative assessment is conducted at the end of the course. In this text OSCE is presented as a method that can be used in both formative and summative assessment. Consistent with the definitions provided earlier, it involves gathering data in a standardized manner through observation and interpretation of those data in relation to clear performance outcome expectations, often defined on a rating scale. These data can be used as feedback to students during a course, in preparation for or during the field practicum, or in planning continuing professional development. Instructors can also use outcome data to identify curriculum areas that need strengthening, content that should be included, and weaknesses in teaching approaches.

The term *evaluation,* which as noted earlier has been used extensively in social work field practica, is defined by the National Academy for Academic Leadership (2013) in relation to their definition of assessment. "Evaluation uses information based on the credible evidence generated through assessment to make judgments of relative value: the acceptability of the conditions described through assessment." For the purposes of this text, evaluation involves the assignment of relative value to an assessment (as defined earlier) such as a grade or final mark as to the acceptability of performance as compared with a benchmark or scale. The process of assessment (measuring student learning through credible evidence) is undertaken to improve student learning or program effectiveness. The evaluation component of this process assigns a value to the findings in terms of their acceptability in relation to the standards that have been set, such as a grade standard assigned to an assessment score or a minimum benchmark assigned for a student to pass the field practicum.

Although educational outcome assessment or assessment of competence is difficult, social work educators are creating innovative approaches that are authentic, reliable, and valid (see the special 2011 issue of the journal *Social Work Education: The International Journal, 30*[2]). Based on the view of competence provided in this chapter, the challenge for social work educators is to design assessment methods and tools that accommodate the multifaceted dimensions of competence and more closely align and link knowledge, cognitive and subjective capacity, practice behaviors, and skill.

We designed, tested, and refined an OSCE adapted for social work (Bogo, Regehr, Logie, et al., 2011) to achieve this goal. Based on our model of holistic competence, discussed earlier in this chapter, it appeared that an OSCE could be used to assess multiple components of competence related to engaging in a collaborative relationship, conducting assessments, and jointly developing intervention goals (Bogo et al., 2013). By adding a reflective activity we were able to also assess conceptualization of practice, which is the way students integrate, use, or apply social work knowledge in understanding their practice and the scenario, including how students think about diversity and engage it in practice. Connected is the nature of students' cognitive processing, critical thinking, and whether students could articulate the links between social work knowledge, values, and their judgments and decision-making process. Through reflection we could also assess intentional use of self and self-regulation, which is students' awareness of their subjective emotional reactions to the client situation and how they managed their emotions in the interview. We aimed to assess students' capacity to reflect on thoughts, feelings, and reactions in practice and use reflection and self-regulation to guide practice. Another dimension involved assessing the ways in which students extract learning from reflecting on their performance and identify future goals based on this analysis. (Rating scales developed for assessment of students based on this conceptualization of holistic competence can be found in Appendix B.)

OSCEs involve the use of standardized patients or clients who are trained to simulate and enact a clinical situation in a consistent, standardized, reliable, and valid fashion. These client situations are designed to be authentic and similar to those that might typically be seen by a practitioner. Students are provided with identifying information and then directed to conduct an interview that is rated on a number of competencies by a faculty member or clinical instructor following rating guidelines. The use of standardized simulated clients ensures that the nature of the problem and level of difficulty are the same for all students. The OSCE focuses on students' performance ability in relation to a number of defined competencies.

The OSCE was originally developed to evaluate medical students and residents and currently is used in a wide range of health professions such as nursing (Cant, McKenna, & Cooper, 2013; Jones, Pegram, & Fordham-Clarke, 2010), pharmacy (Austin, O'Byrne, Pugsley, & Quero Munoz, 2003; Sturpe, 2010), midwifery (Govaerts, van der Vleuten, & Schuwirth, 2002), physical therapy (Wessel, Williams, Finch, & Gemus, 2003), dentistry (Graham, Bitzer, & Anderson, 2013; Mossey, Newton, & Stirrups, 2001), and assessing learning in interprofessional care (Simmons et al., 2011). The OSCE provides professional educational programs with the opportunity to assess students' clinical competence through a procedure that involves observing and evaluating students' actual performance (Harden & Gleeson, 1979; Hodges, Hanson, McNaughton, & Regehr, 2002; van der Vleuten & Swanson, 1990). It has wide acceptance in medical schools internationally and in North America because it is standardized with respect to the nature of client problem presented and level of difficulty, and hence fair for students (Harden & Gleeson, 1979). It is also valued for its ability to evaluate clinical competence (Turner & Dankoski, 2008). In a review of the OSCE method over the past three decades, Hodges (2006) cites an extensive research literature that finds that the method has acceptable validity and reliability, is experienced positively by students and faculty members, and is used frequently for episodic performance-based assessment in undergraduate medical education and specialty areas and in licensing examinations in some countries. The effect of OSCE in competence assessment in psychiatry over two decades finds similar positive outcomes (Hodges, Hollenberg, McNaughton, Hanson, & Regehr, 2014).

In social work education, instructors have predominately used experiential teaching approaches such as role play of client situations with student colleagues enacting the role. In a critical review of studies on the use of standardized clients in both classroom instruction and assessment, Logie and colleagues (2013) found 17 studies dating back to the mid-1990s. Although the review found that studies vary in methodological quality and recommended stronger research designs, it noted that the approach is well-received by students and instructors. A number of recent studies informed the work presented in this publication. Rawlings (2012) compared students' performance in a one-scenario OSCE at the beginning and end of an undergraduate program. Using standardized instruments with high internal consistency, the study measured practice skill and self-efficacy. Study findings revealed that mean scores on all scales and subscales were significantly higher for students completing the program than for those beginning, yet self-efficacy was not predictive of skill performance. A separate series of studies conducted over 4 years tested the reliability of the OSCE for Social Work Practice Performance Rating scale and found that internal consistency ranged from α = .71 to .92, with higher levels of internal consistency attained from a 5-point scale than from a 3-point scale (Rawlings & Johnson, 2011). Interrater reliability was also assessed for 3 of the 4 years, with 2 years demonstrating a significant intraclass correlation coefficient and with 1 year demonstrating no correlation, suggesting high variation between raters. As anchor descriptors were added, correlation improved. There was also consistently high agreement between raters on a single item rating overall performance of the students, suggesting the importance of including an overall performance item on a practice performance rating scale (Rawlings & Johnson, 2011).

To test the validity of the OSCE for Social Work Practice Performance Rating Scale, scores were examined to determine whether they predicted performance on field evaluation performance the next year. Despite small sample sizes, under simple regression techniques the overall performance item on the OSCE was found to be predictive of performance on the field evaluation instrument (p < .05), with the total mean score of the scale approaching significance (p = .06) (Rawlings & Johnson, 2012). These findings suggest that carefully constructed OSCE measures have the potential to assist us in determining student readiness for field education.

An OSCE was developed and used to assess master's degree students' clinical competence and cultural sensitivity on the completion of a course on clinical practice with diversity (Lu et al., 2011). The researchers identified 10 categories: "professional values, knowledge, cultural empathy, interviewing skills, intervention skills, empowerment perspectives, critical thinking, professional use of self, evaluations and knowledge of legal mandates" (Lu et al., 2011, p. 174). These categories were subsequently placed into four groups with behavioral indicators to guide rating of nine levels of performance. The resulting categories were interviewing skills, cultural empathy, assessment and intervention, and comprehensive evaluation. Six standardized client situations were designed to include diversity in age, gender, race, religion, sexual orientation, and socioeconomic status. A total of 101 students conducted interviews, which were rated by the course instructors. The rating scale developed for the study demonstrated high internal consistency, and the authors recommend it as a potentially useful instrument for assessing student performance using an OSCE.

Bogo, Regehr, Logie, and colleagues (2011) developed and tested a five-scenario OSCE consisting of a performance interview followed by a reflective dialogue to assess students' holistic competence. This OSCE was administered to 11 master's students at the end of the first year, seven students who had completed the second year, and five experienced practitioners. The study found promising reliability of each rating tool comparable to, although slightly lower than, those in related health professions. The method also demonstrated construct validity in that it could differentiate between experienced practitioners and students. Of special interest was the observation that students' scores were generally in the midrange of the rating scales, in comparison to the high ratings reported in the literature and anecdotally on field evaluations. Finally, regardless of the scenario participants began in when taking the OSCE, their scores on both the performance and reflection scales improved, demonstrating that participants were actually learning through the experience of performing and reflecting. This occurred despite the absence of any feedback in this study from the rater or actor, as well as being rated by different raters for each scenario. This pilot serves as a proof-of-concept study, and its results can encourage social work educators to conduct further research and experimentation with the method.

Stimulated by these promising findings, an OSCE was integrated as the final examination at the end of a first-term integrated practice course and skill laboratory for first-year master's students. In this program students enter the field practicum in their second term. There were 125 students in the program requiring modification of the OSCE method due to resource constraints. Students participated in only one scenario, and rather than a dialogue, reflections were written in response to the standardized questions. This adaptation of the OSCE method was tested and yielded important results (Bogo et al., 2012). First, striking variation in students' scores indicated that the scales were able to capture differences in students' competence. Also, as noted, "correlational analyses revealed an association between OSCE scales and field final evaluations" (p. 428). However, although all students who had difficulty in the field also had lower scores in the OSCE, not all students who had lower scores on the OSCE did poorly in the field. We speculated that reasons for this discrepancy could be related to performance anxiety on the OSCE, to students' learning and growth through the practicum, or to students having greater comfort with the practicum population and issues than with those in the OSCE scenario. When these findings were presented to field instructors, however, they thought that the discrepancy probably resulted from the lack of observation of student performance by field instructors who are responsible for student field evaluations. They commented that field instructors often rate students based on written and verbal reports in the context of their relationships with their field instructors, an observation supported in the literature (Maidment, 2000; Rogers & McDonald, 1995). We speculated that the field instructor ratings of students on field evaluations in our study may actually be more indicative of the quality of students' meta-competencies (e.g., how they conceptualize their practice and how they discuss their subjective experiences) than of their actual performance. This speculation is supported by the study finding that the main associations between the OSCE scores and the field evaluations were found on the subscales related to meta-competencies rather than on the subscales related to performance.

Forgey, Badger, Gilbert, and Hansen (2013) reported on a study using standardized clients to train army civilian social workers and to evaluate the effectiveness of the curriculum to teach them to assess intimate partner violence. Increases were found in participants' knowledge, ability to explore critical content, and interviewing skills. These authors note that the use of standardized clients to teach effective evidence-based assessment methods is beneficial, especially when questions of safety are present. In situations where there is a danger of harming others, such as in this example of intimate partner violence and in cases of child maltreatment or of self-harm and suicide, social workers need opportunities to learn and to practice assessment skills. The researchers strongly advocate the use of standardized clients "in these situations [where] the consequences of failing to explore a key area of inquiry and accurately assess the level of risk could be lethal" (Forgey et al., 2013, p. 304). Yet a recent scoping review of the use of simulation in training child welfare workers to assess maltreatment in children at risk found few studies that use this method (Bogo, Shlonsky, Lee, & Serbinski, 2014).

In summary, there is widespread evidence and acceptance of the effectiveness of using simulated clients in teaching and simulated standardized client scenarios in OSCEs to assess student learning in health professions education. A growing community of social work educators and researchers are adapting, developing, and studying its use in social work, with promising results. As we develop and test educational and assessment methods we can identify critical factors that lead to better student mastery of competence and in turn refine our teaching and evaluation of learning outcomes.

Reflection and the OSCE

Returning to our conceptualization of holistic competence, we recognized that this complex view required a holistic assessment strategy, one that would capture the various components involved in competent practice. The usual OSCE method of observing and rating students' performance with standardized clients could be used to assess the way students actually performed in their use of procedural competencies. Literature on assessment, across disciplines, underscores the imperative of observing practice if one aims to assess competence. However, simply observing practice does not necessarily provide access to components such as the meta-competencies that inform performance and the demonstration of practice behaviors. For example, as noted earlier, in the Toronto study we were interested in the way in which students conceptualize their practice and use the knowledge taught in courses to guide their actions, how students think about diversity and engage it in practice, and how they exercise judgment and process their internal emotional states (Bogo et al., 2006, 2013). These components of competence are integrated throughout the proposed EPAS 2015 (CSWE, 2014). An additional method was needed; a reflective activity linked to the performance was chosen to elicit information that would assist in assessment of these components.

Reflection as a method of accessing implicit or tacit knowledge has been extensively discussed in literature on education for professional practice in general as well as in social work. Reflection was described by Dewey (1933) in educational theory and popularized by Kolb (1984) in adult education and management education. Donald Schon (1983, 1987) related reflection to professional practice in his argument that professional work is more than technical rationality, involving the application of rigorous specialized knowledge to problems confronted by practitioners. Technical rationality pays little attention to the ways in which practitioners' own perceptions, values, and personal attributes affect the way in which they define and frame problems and how they choose and provide interventions. Technical rationality implies that practitioners are neutral, even-handed, and not active players in constructing and making meaning of problem situations. In contrast, Schon (1987) proposed that practitioners use tacit knowledge or *knowing-in-action* to work with the unique and complex situations they confront through a process of reflective practice in which they "reflect in the midst of action without interrupting it" (p. 26). When practitioners are confronted with situations that contain an element of surprise or do not respond to usual procedures, a reflective–active process may come into play, "thinking [that] serves to reshape what we are doing while we are doing it. I shall say, in cases like this, that we *reflect-in-action*" (p. 26). He describes this reflection as considering the phenomena confronted, using critical thinking, and questioning our assumptions. Ideally this type of reflection leads to reconsidering the way the situation was framed or understood and in turn arriving at new strategies for action. This reflection occurs while one is in the practice situation and therefore provides the chance for self-correction and experimentation with new actions. These actions may produce intended results or may stimulate the need for further reflection and subsequent new actions. Reflection-in-action is nonlinear, probably not deliberative, but happens in the process. Experience, wisdom, and insight operate in a way that allows flexibility in framing and reframing the problem and using creativity and improvisation in trying new responses. A method to study this reflection in the moment has not yet been described in the literature on social work or related human service professions.

For Schon another feature of professional practice is *reflection-on-action,* in which practitioners look back on their practice and critically review it (Schon, 1983). The aim is to reexamine the situation and the professionals' experience of the event and thoughts about it, including some evaluation of what transpired and what actions were or were not successful. Ideally, through reflection practitioners can learn from the experience so that an element of self-correction for future interactions with the case is introduced, new learning in general can be added to one's repertoire, and needed new information is identified to pursue in professional development. Reflection on its own rests on the practitioner's memory and recall, including one's perceptions, and is a manifestation of the practitioner's own view of reality. Schon (1987) observes that practitioners have difficulty when they try to report on what they know and why they did what they did. As others have noted, practitioners' accounts of the rationale for particular actions and judgments, also called practice wisdom, have eluded concrete definition and explication and are difficult to study (Bogo, Regehr, et al., 2004; Eraut, 2002).

As we considered how to access and assess meta-competencies using an OSCE, it became apparent that a structured reflection activity conducted immediately after the simulated interview held promise as an innovative assessment method. Reflective activities reported in social work education literature usually rely on written or verbal student self-report of situations they choose to consider. For example, Boud and Knights (1996) recommend using journal writing or sharing experiences with a fellow student, a learning partner, to focus on what the student has learned and how this might influence her or his practice, as well as using self-assessment protocols. In all these examples students' reflections are based on experiences that the instructor or rater has not seen. This means that students choose which aspects of situations they will focus on and which they will ignore. Also, given distortions in recall, the teacher is actually assessing material that is one step removed from what may actually have transpired in the practice situation.

Although we are interested in gaining access to both dimensions of reflection, in action and on action, as others have noted (Eraut, 2004; Rogers, 2001) it is difficult to research reflection in action. Instead, a reflective activity was chosen and added immediately after the simulated interview to assess students' internal cognitive processes, subjective experiences, and emotional reactions. The focus was on how students identified and processed their thoughts and feelings and how this was linked to their performance in the interview.

Rather than a free-flowing discussion, we developed probes for postinterview reflection, following the procedures of Barrows (2000b) for stimulated recall. The goal was to use the performance in the interview as the focus and stimulus for reflection. There is extensive discussion about reflective practice, but there are no reports of systematic standardized reflections on a student's specific performance in the social work literature. Using our model of holistic competence in social work, the reflection activity was designed to explore four dimensions of meta-competence: the way students conceptualize their practice and what theories and practice models were used to understand the client and guide students' behavior in the simulation; the way students engaged with difference, as each scenario presented multiple factors related to diversity that needed to be taken into account; the way students dealt with personal reactions to the simulation and maintained a professional and intentional use of self; and what students felt confident about and what they felt they needed to learn before seeing a client similar to the one portrayed in the simulation. In one study an interview with the student was conducted by the rater following a set of questions and rated on a reflection scale immediately after the student interview with the standardized client (Bogo, Regehr, Katz, et al., 2011). In a subsequent and larger study, students wrote reflections immediately after the interview with the standardized client in response to the set of questions on a computer. These responses were subsequently rated by the examiner on the reflection scale (Katz, Tufford, Bogo, & Regehr, 2014).

Qualitative analysis of the reflections in the studies also revealed variation in students' abilities on the components that were assessed. For each component a continuum was found, from in-depth, rich, and textured responses to more superficial, scant, and concrete discussion. The ability to conceptualize practice and use the theories and principles taught in social work programs was linked to students' subjective reactions; for some students difficulty managing emotional self-regulation left them unable to use their knowledge base or perform effectively in the interview (Bogo et al., 2013; Katz et al., 2014).

Typically, reflective activities in social work education in courses and field education use journal entries, written papers, or process records that ask students to reflect on an experience or a segment of practice sometime after the event. However, the instructor rarely views the practice situation and therefore has no authentic appreciation of the content or performance subjected to analysis. The reflections are based exclusively on recall of a practice situation and include the student's own report of her perceptions of how she performed. A body of literature in medicine, nursing, and experimental settings has found a negative relationship between self-assessment and performance (Baxter & Norman, 2011; Davis et al., 2006; Eva & Regehr, 2005). Some weaker performers tend to overrate themselves, and some stronger performers tend to rate themselves as less capable than they actually were.

The unique features of the OSCE adapted for social work are that it includes a reflection that links various components of competence, is based on the student's actual performance, and occurs immediately after the interview. As a result, when raters assess the reflection they do so in light of the interview that has just been conducted. Though not systematically analyzed, a number of raters reported that some students' reflections included statements about actions they believed they had taken in the interview. However, the raters did not see any evidence of these actions that students described. In discussion, the raters did not think the students were not being truthful; rather, they speculated that the human tendency to reconstruct events in a way that one thought or wished had occurred may account for this discrepancy.

Sidebars 1 and 2 illustrate the sequence of activity in a traditional OSCE and in the OSCE adapted for social work. Video recordings that illustrate the various steps can be accessed at http://youtu.be/vFSd9D6PF18 and http://youtu.be/JMvsgNVBrtk. Variations and additions to these procedures have included using the rating scale for student self-assessment. If the examiner wants to expand the reflection and include a lengthier written assignment, the interview can be video recorded and used by the student to conduct an analysis following the instructor's particular directions. Assignments using this method will be discussed in a later chapter and can be found in Appendix D. In Chapter 2, specific procedures and considerations for designing the various aspects of the OSCE are presented.

Sidebar 1

Typical OSCE Procedure

1. The student receives a brief, one-paragraph, written introduction to the scenario that sets the context for the interaction. Students are given about 1 minute to read this statement.

2. The student conducts a 12- to 15-minute interview with a simulated standardized client while one or more examiners observe and assess the performance on a rating scale.

3. If there is more than one scenario, the student proceeds to the next scenario.

Sidebar 2

The OSCE Adapted for Social Work Procedure

1. The student receives a brief, one-paragraph, written introduction to the scenario that sets the context for the interaction. Students are given about 1 minute to read this statement.

2. The student conducts a 12- to 15-minute interview with a simulated standardized client while one or more examiners observe and assess the performance on a rating scale.

3. The standardized client is trained to provide up to 5 minutes of verbal feedback to the student, or the standardized client can provide written feedback to the student.

4. The rater provides up to 5 minutes of verbal feedback, or the rater can provide written feedback to the student.

5. A 15- to 25-minute directed reflection activity is conducted, either a structured discussion between the candidate and the examiner or a structured written reflection about specific dimensions of the student's performance.

CHAPTER 2

Designing an Objective Structured Clinical Examination (OSCE)

Designing an OSCE is a very interesting process and can feel challenging the first time one approaches the task. And if they are available, we recommend a team of colleagues with an interest in education, education research, and social work practice. Developing an OSCE can also be done in smaller social work programs, such as with instructors who are teaching sections of the same course. This chapter outlines the critical aspects of developing strong, reliable, and valid examinations using simulation with standardized clients. Our work benefitted from input from scholars in medical education research and cognitive science, social work doctoral students, experienced social work field instructors and practitioners, standardized clients, and the standardized client trainers at the local medical school. In our initial efforts to develop an OSCE for social work, we were guided by the blueprint provided by Hodges and colleagues (Hodges et al., 2002), who recommend creating a "matrix that outlines parameters for the examination: content areas, knowledge, skills and attitudes, station type, and length" (p. 143). They also recommend that the content of the OSCE reflect the content of the curriculum. We soon found it necessary to develop our own understanding of the various aspects of the examination for social work. This may be because of medicine's emphasis on accessing specific information (e.g., conducting an interview to obtain a history and description of particular symptoms to arrive at a diagnosis), in contrast to social work's more complex view of practice (e.g., when interviewing we may use empathy and genuineness to build a relationship, which facilitates eliciting facts about the presenting problem, the person, and the situation and information about relevant systems and the client's emotional responses). In medicine the OSCE generally includes a checklist with details of what the student should complete, and the evaluator or standardized client checks one of two choices: The student did this, or the student did not do this. We decided that this approach does not capture the holistic view of competence in social work practice as presented in Chapter 1. It also does not reflect the way in which content is elicited through an interactive and collaborative process between the practitioner and the client.

As a result, the development of an OSCE for social work involved, to some extent, forging our own path and at times retracing our steps, learning through trial and error. We expect that most instructors and teams will have this experience as well. The back-and-forth process helped us continually clarify what we were trying to assess and whether our curriculum and course content provided enough opportunity for students to learn and master the competencies at the expected level. In this way, designing the OSCE served as a feedback loop for continuous quality improvement of our curriculum and program. However, it was at times challenging and difficult. As we continue to develop new projects and additional scenarios, the process has become clearer because we are building on what we have learned in earlier phases. We share our experiences and the steps to take in the interests of helping others use and experiment with this effective method of assessment.

Four processes are involved in OSCE development (Figure 2). The first and perhaps most challenging step is to conceptualize the social work competencies one is seeking to assess and the related practice behaviors that can be observable indicators of those competencies. For schools accredited by the CSWE, the competency framework provides the overall blueprint, although programs can add to it. The second process is mapping the competencies (and related practice behaviors) in relation to a potential scenario, highlighting the client issues and the related student abilities to include in the third step, designing scenarios. Scenarios must be developed to include material for students to respond to and demonstrate in their performance of the competencies and identified practice behaviors. The fourth step is creating a rating scale that spells out in more specific behavioral terms what the student should demonstrate in the interview. The process involves moving between levels of abstraction toward defining more grounded actions that can be assessed in an OSCE.

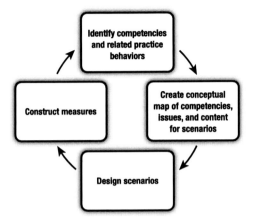

Figure 2. Iterative process for developing the OSCE.

This chapter presents guidance based on what we have learned about this process through delivering and testing OSCEs. Unfortunately, the presentation is offered in a linear fashion, whereas our work was highly iterative, with each developmental step leading to further changes in earlier activities and methods (see Figure 2). As additional scenarios were created, our understanding of competence and how it could be assessed became clearer.

The following section presents the stages and recommended associated tasks for developing OSCEs, with examples drawn from our work.

Identify Competencies and Associated Practice Behaviors

The first step in creating an OSCE is to identify which competencies will be measured and to begin to identify the related practice behaviors. EPAS 2015 (CSWE, 2014) notes, "Practice often requires the performance of multiple competencies simultaneously; therefore, assessment of those competencies may optimally be carried out at the same time" (p. 22). The OSCE can therefore serve as an efficient method and provide assessment and a measure for a number of competencies and practice behaviors.

We began our work before CSWE's 2008 EPAS and used our developing conceptualization of competence, discussed in Chapter 1, to guide the design. This conceptualization maps well onto the EPAS 2008 framework and we expect will be useful as well in EPAS 2015 (CSWE, 2014). The EPAS framework can also be used to address competencies for specialized areas of practice. Some examples of the relationship between Draft 2 of the EPAS competencies and the conceptualization used in the OSCE Adapted for Social Work are presented in Table 1 to illustrate links between various definitions of competencies and related practice behaviors.

Table 1. EPAS Competencies and Practice Behaviors and Holistic Competence Model Used in the OSCE Adapted for Social Work: Selected Examples

Draft 2/2015 EPAS Competencies and Practice Behaviors	Holistic Competence Model (Bogo et al., 2011, 2012, 2013)
1. Demonstrate ethical and professional behavior: • Make ethical decisions by applying the standards of the NASW Code of Ethics, relevant laws and regulations, models for ethical decision making, and additional codes of ethics as appropriate to context. • Use reflection and self-regulation to manage personal values and maintain professionalism in practice situations.	• Conceptualization of practice • Intentional use of self and self-regulation • Learning
2. Engage diversity and difference in practice: • Present themselves as learners and engage client systems as experts of their own experiences. • Apply self-awareness and self-regulation to manage the influence of personal biases and values in working with diverse client systems.	• Conceptualization of practice • Engaging diversity • Intentional use of self and self-regulation • Relationship building
4. Engage in practice-informed research and research-informed practice: • Use and translate research findings to inform and improve practice, policy, and service delivery.	• Conceptualization of practice
5. Engage in policy practice: • Assess how social welfare and economic policies impact the delivery of and access to social services.	• Conceptualization of practice • Assessment

(continued)

Table 1 (continued)

6. Engage with individuals, families, groups, organizations, and communities: • Apply knowledge of human behavior and the social environment and practice context to engage with client systems. • Use empathy, self-regulation, and interpersonal skills to effectively engage diverse client systems.	• Conceptualization of practice • Intentional use of self and self-regulation • Relationship building • Engaging diversity
7. Assess individuals, families, groups, organizations, and communities: • Collect, organize, and critically analyze and interpret information from client systems. • Apply knowledge of human behavior and the social environment, person-in-environment, and other multidisciplinary theoretical frameworks in the assessment of data from client systems. • Develop mutually agreed-on intervention goals and objectives based on the critical assessment of strengths, needs, and challenges within client systems. • Select appropriate intervention strategies based on the assessment, research knowledge, and values and preferences of client systems.	• Conceptualization of practice • Intentional use of self and self-regulation • Engaging diversity • Relationship building • Assessment • Planning and goal setting
8. Intervene with individuals, families, groups, organizations, and communities: • Implement interventions to achieve practice goals and enhance capacities of client systems. • Apply knowledge of human behavior and the social environment, person-in-environment, and other multidisciplinary theoretical frameworks in interventions with client systems.	• Conceptualization of practice • Intentional use of self and self-regulation • Engaging diversity • Relationship building

When beginning to think about creating an OSCE for social work, educators must consider a number of issues. First is the way in which they will work with the relevant accreditation framework and expectations in their particular country to identify the competencies, practice behaviors, and indicators of the competency that could be assessed in an OSCE. A competence framework is useful for social work educators internationally and provides guidance for designing OSCEs. Competence will be understood in relation to the mission and goals of the educational program and related to the respective accreditation framework. For example, for social work programs in the United States the relevant framework is that provided by the CSWE EPAS (2008, 2014). In England the Professional Capability Framework (CSW, 2012a) is similar in many respects to that used in EPAS 2008, although it relates to expectations of social workers not only on graduation but also throughout their professional careers. In Canadian schools of social work the goals of educational programs are expressed as learning objectives. The Toronto team's original work was in a Canadian school. The process of identifying competencies associated with the broad objectives in the Canadian Association for Social Work Education Standards for Accreditation (CASWE-ACFTS, 2013) provided us with an effective way of articulating and assessing the dimensions that constituted a number of the general objectives.

The second issue to consider is the purpose of the OSCE. For example, will the OSCE be used as one assessment measure in a one-semester course, at midterm, or as the final assignment? An OSCE can also be used to assess learning at the end of a segment of the program, for example, before beginning practicum in an undergraduate program, in a delayed practicum-entry master's program, or for advanced-standing students to assess readiness to begin the practicum and to obtain a baseline of their competence level. The OSCE can also be used as an exit assessment at the completion of the entire program and designed in a way to capture many of the competencies expected for graduation.

An OSCE can also be used to assess competence in specialized practice. For example, because competencies for a number of specialized areas have already been developed (see *Advanced Gero Social Work Practice* [CSWE, 2008], *Advanced Social Work Practice in Military Social Work* [CSWE, 2010], *Advanced Social Work Practice in Trauma* [CSWE, 2012], *Advanced Practice in Clinical Social Work* [CSWE, 2009], *Advanced Practice in Macro Social Work* [ACOSA, 2013]), conceptual work exists that can be used to guide the design of scenarios and rating scales. The selected competencies must reflect the areas of specialized practice, be aligned to the competencies in EPAS, and be designed in relation to the purpose and weight given to students' performance in the OSCE.

When professions adopt a competency framework, new applicants to educational programs may seek credit for prior learning gained in other countries, in similar human service educational programs, or in paraprofessional employment. Indeed, OSCE is used in medicine and nursing to assess the competence of internationally educated health professionals wanting to practice in Ontario, Canada. The Centre for the Evaluation of Health Professionals Educated Abroad (2011) states, regarding testing of medical doctors,

> Our standardized evaluations help to level the playing field for IMGs [international medical graduate] candidates. The exams ensure that they meet the standards for Canadian training and practice, they allow them to compare their clinical competencies with those of Canadian medical graduates and they improve their chances of obtaining residency positions.

Having used the accreditation framework and purpose of the OSCE to identify competencies and practice behaviors to be assessed, the next step is to ensure that students have had the opportunity to learn the competencies. A diagram can be used to map linkages between the competencies, practice behaviors, content in one or more courses, and learning activities. Instructors can choose specific competencies and then define practice behaviors at varying levels from general to specific, from broad to detailed skill sets. More fine-grained definitions of practice behaviors will occur as rating scales are developed, a topic that will be discussed further in this chapter. At this point it is useful to focus on practice behaviors at a middle level of specificity. For example, regarding Competency 6 in Draft 2 of EPAS, "Engagement," a practice behavior is to "use empathy, self-regulation, and interpersonal skills to effectively engage diverse client systems" (CSWE, 2014, p. 6). This is a sufficient definition at this point; however, when the rating scale is constructed it will be necessary to define these behaviors in far more detailed ways so that they can be assessed. Similarly, for Competency 2, "Engage diversity and difference in practice," a practice behavior is, "present themselves as learners and engage client systems as experts of their own experiences" (CSWE, 2014, p. 4). This description will benefit from further specification of components and related indicators or behaviors to guide ratings during the assessment. It is important to acknowledge the inherent tension in assessing complex social work tasks with the need to specify behaviors that can be observed and assessed. One needs a balance between a behavior that is too broad to be measured and one that is so specific that it does not allow nuanced performance that authentically captures the essence of the competency.

Competency-based education is aimed at creating educational approaches that lead to students' mastery of competencies. As a result, instructors must work backwards: Once an end competence is identified, instructors must decide on the substantive content and learning activities that will contribute to students' educational experiences so that they can master the knowledge, skills, attitudes, and abilities that, taken together, will produce the desired competency. For example, the competency "Assessment" requires exposure to and mastery of a social work approach, such as the ecosystem framework, to provide a guide and focus for the practice behaviors involved in information gathering. Students also must use interviewing skills effectively to enable preliminary engagement and connection so that a client may respond to open- and closed-ended questions used by the student to elicit relevant information. Students will also need to develop awareness of their own cognitive processes and subjective reactions. As discussed in Chapter 1, competent social workers appreciate the need for self-awareness of the ways in which they analyze client information and the factors that influence their critical thinking about information collected. These factors include their tacit knowledge and subjective reactions based on a wide range of personal and professional experiences. Because social work assessments guide planning and intervention, educators view competence in this area as crucial for effective practice. These various components of holistic competence can be taught in a range of courses, including those focusing on theory, research, practice, in an interviewing skills course or laboratory, and also in the field. Assessment of learning in each of these courses could involve use of an OSCE, or one OSCE could provide an examination to assess the students' integration of all the elements of knowledge, skill, and analytical abilities across all of these courses and in the field. Either way, content on the knowledge, skills, and attitudes must be delivered so that students are prepared to execute the competency in such a way that it can be assessed.

Once competencies are identified, instructors will need to consider which particular competencies can be reasonably assessed in short interview segments conducted with simulated standardized clients. In a short segment generally there will be opportunities to view students' performance in the early stage of a practice interview, including information gathering, relationship building, and preliminary assessment. There may be aspects of planning for intervention that can also be examined. Specific skill sets, such as assessing for child abuse or substance abuse, could also be assessed in this format. In health professions education, specific topics have been taught and assessed using simulated and standardized clients, such as breaking bad news and responding to angry clients. However, it is important to avoid assessing too many competencies in one interview segment; trying to do too much in one scenario makes it difficult for students to perform all the competencies you are looking for and also makes it harder for the rater to observe accurately.

It is likely to be more difficult to assess change process interventions using the OSCE method because the OSCE generally involves student interviews of short duration, approximately 15 minutes. However, creative case development might allow certain aspects of intervention to be elicited and assessed. For example, a number of segments in one client situation could be developed, with students receiving information about progress after an initial interview and after a few more meetings with the client. Instructions would be provided to students about what has already been accomplished and what processes or tasks should be demonstrated in the subsequent simulated interview. The format presented in this chapter is that of a 15-minute OSCE, which introduces the constraint of time. We have found that these interviews can provide enough data about student performance to yield a reasonable assessment of certain aspects of competence. It is surprising how much one can observe in a short segment.

Depending on the purpose of the OSCE, student competencies may need to be assessed across several different case scenarios (also called stations in the medical literature). Generally, higher-stakes tests, such as comprehensive evaluations, or evaluations that may determine a student's progression in a program require more OSCE stations (three to five) to allow a valid assessment of the student's skill. Depending on these considerations, instructors will decide on the number of scenarios considered necessary and fair to assess mastery. Resource implications will certainly be a part of these decisions.

Create a Conceptual Map of Competencies, Issues, and Content

Once the instructor has identified the competencies, related practice behaviors, and some indicators for rating when assessing, working iteratively, the specific issues for each case must be developed to provide students the opportunity to demonstrate the practice behaviors related to the competency. That is, standardized client scenarios must be constructed so that actors will portray and offer relevant content that enables students to respond or probe for more information in a way that allows competence to be assessed on the various dimensions. The case example of Mrs. Gonzales (Appendix C) can illustrate these points. The key competencies to be assessed were (1) engagement in a collaborative relationship (similar to Competency 6, Draft 2 EPAS 2015 "Engage"), (2) demonstrates cultural competence (similar to Competency 2, Draft 2 EPAS 2015 "Engage Diversity and Difference"), and (3) conduct an ecosystemic assessment (similar to Competency 7, Draft 2 EPAS 2015 "Assess"). The practice behaviors associated with these competencies were further specified as indicators so that they could be assessed. For the competency of "Engagement," students were required to demonstrate that they could develop a collaborative relationship by clearly introducing themselves and their role, asking for and responding to specific issues in the situation and to the client's feelings, demonstrating empathy and sensitivity, and helping the client express her needs and feelings. For the competency of "Engage Diversity," students were expected to explore cultural cues and content to understand this dimension of the client's life and how it gave meaning to the client's experiences and to the range of possible solutions. For the "Assess" competency, students were expected to conduct an ecosystemic assessment and to explore the presenting problem, the relevant social networks, and the strengths and to begin to set the stage for collaborative goal setting. Conceptual mapping, as shown in Table 2, provides examples of the links made between some of the competencies, practice behaviors, indicators for rating, and specific dimensions or issues that are expected to be addressed in each scenario.

For each scenario it is useful to brainstorm and arrive at the specific issue and content. Issues are the particular case-related concerns that students should address as evidence of their ability on the broader competency dimensions. In the case of Mrs. Gonzales, the precipitant was the death of the father of the family and the referral from the school as the son's grades were deteriorating. Emotional distress was predominant, with sadness and grief, along with concrete challenges regarding the loss of the primary breadwinner and related financial needs, practical arrangements for care of the children, gender roles and new expectations for the young son, and cultural issues. Table 2 illustrates these ideas for five cases, all of which can be found in Appendix C.

Design Scenarios
Draft a Case Scenario
Once competencies and practice behaviors have been drafted in their initial form (they will be modified as the iterative process of case development unfolds) and case content linked, the next phase of drafting the case scenario occurs. Larger universities, especially those with a medical school, are likely to have a standardized patient program with simulation educators and a standardized patient trainer who can assist in case development and in the overall use of this method. Smaller universities can draw on the expertise of acting coaches, faculty, and experienced social workers. Similar to Miller's (2004) work in social work, the faculty member must be actively involved in developing the scenario. After working with the standardized patient program on three scenarios, we were able to develop and refine additional scenarios on our own.

For social work educators working alone, we suggest beginning case development with brainstorming about the potential client issues and student tasks, as discussed earlier. It is extremely useful to consult experienced social workers who work with similar situations and in relevant settings. These workers can examine whether the scenarios represent individuals and families they see in their practice and provide additional suggestions for authenticity in the scenarios. If portraying a particular cultural group, it is also helpful to consult members of that population for feedback on accurate portrayal of the cultural dimensions of the case scenario that you want to present.

As scenarios are written it is crucial to constantly refer to the performance expectations or learning outcomes of the related course or program segment and consider two issues. First, have students been taught the competencies,

Table 2. Conceptual Mapping of Competencies in Social Work OSCEs: A Guide for Developing and Conceptualizing Case Scenarios							
Competency and Practice Behaviors	Indicator for Rating	Specific Client Domains	Case Scenarios				
			Case 1: Mrs. Gonzales	Case 2: Simone	Case 3: Mr. Phillips	Case 4: Mary Peters	Case 5: Natalya
Engage and use empathy	Demonstrates empathy and sensitivity; helps the client express her needs and feelings through appropriate verbal feedback and nonverbal expressions	Emotional distress	Husband's death	Coping with sexuality	Injury, financial stress, family obligation	Loneliness and physical health issues	Loneliness, isolation, anxiety, anger
		Physical distress	n/a	n/a	Client in visible distress due to injury	Client suffers pain with arthritis; impact on mobility and activities of daily living	Fatigue and lack of sleep; weight loss due to sporadic eating
Engage diversity and self as learner	Explores cultural cues and content for understanding; able to elicit and affirm cultural identity	Culture, class, and ethnicity	Low-income cultural adjustment as Mexican immigrant	Perception of sexuality in Jamaican and Canadian culture	Working-class white Anglo-Saxon male identity	Older white Anglo-Saxon identity	Low-income newcomer from Russia
		Gender	Transition from at-home mother into workforce; son's gendered discomfort with role of babysitter	Disconnection with peer heterosexual gender norms	Compromised identity being a man experiencing inability to work	Identity as older single woman	Identity as young mother with difficulty coping
		Sexual orientation	Heterosexual widow	Difficulty accepting same-sex attraction in context of homophobia	Identity as heterosexual man in a relationship where he is not the primary breadwinner	Identity as a never-married woman	Identity as heterosexual married woman
		Age	Transition to workforce in midlife	Youth attending school; easily affected by peer norms	Midlife work crisis	75-year-old woman facing issues of ageism	26-year-old woman

Assess and conduct ecosystemic assessment — Identifies the relevant systems and social networks (nuclear family, extended family, neighbors, friends, employment, school)						
	Family	Husband died; son who has been having difficulty; 2 other daughters	Parents, siblings in Toronto; extended family in Jamaica	Wife and 2 children	No contact with surviving brother; other siblings dead	Parent and 3 siblings in Russia; husband only family in Canada
	School and work	Was at home until husband's death, then returned to workforce working as unskilled laborer	Grades dropping; not attending school	Wife is a school teacher; he works as an office manager in a small company; children take care of themselves after school	Retired school teacher, no social contacts	Worked as a part-time store clerk until baby's birth; was also taking English classes
	Religion	Not mentioned by client	Very important but a cause of concern because of views on homosexuality	Not mentioned by client	A churchgoer when more mobile	Catholic Church-attended when in Russia
	Community supports	Potential: Latino agencies, supports for widows, school supports for son	Potential: lesbian and gay youth groups, school counselor, gay-positive churches	Potential: school teachers, children's sports, friends, work colleagues	Potential: social support at church, former colleagues, community groups	Potential: Catholic church, newcomer agency, mothers' groups, Russian community

Note: Adapted from Bogo, Logie, & Katz (2009).

practice behaviors, and related content needed to conduct this interview as the scenarios are portrayed? For example, a scenario with potential suicidal ideation was ultimately deemed too difficult to be used for assessment of performance for beginning students who did not have the knowledge to guide a suicide risk assessment interview. However, it could be used to assess more advanced students and also as an effective way of using simulation to teach this content. Second, given the format of the short interview, an OSCE may be suitable for assessing only some of the course competencies, and other assessment methods may be needed for other competencies. As noted, it lends itself well to beginning phases of practice; creativity and innovation are needed to design ways of delivering preliminary information so that it can be used in middle stages to assess intervention competencies.

After brainstorming, the next step is writing a first draft of the client scenario, which will provide information for training the actor to perform the role, including improvisation as the interview proceeds. As part of case development, it is critical to develop verbatim statements (word-for-word quotations) that will be delivered by the actor during the interview to prompt the student on the key aspects of the case. (Examples of verbatim statements are provided in the descriptions of each case, found in Appendix C.) These statements are presented each time the case is enacted and are of the utmost importance because they provide the standardization for the scenario. Standardization gives all students equal opportunity to address the core issues and in turn allows them to demonstrate the practice behavior to be measured. Thus, the standard experience provides a fair test for all participants.

The template presented in Sidebar 3 has proven useful in training numerous standardized clients. Although the scenarios contain critical information for the actor to use in portraying the case, it is important to note that it is impossible to develop a case that will prepare the actor for every question a student might ask. The scenario provides the basic background information, but the actor must be skilled enough to improvise as needed, building on the information provided and in response to students' effective use of skills.

Sidebar 3

Template for Designing Scenarios and Training Standardized Clients

History and Background Information

History of the presenting problem includes demographic information such as gender, age, and ethnicity. Because diversity issues can be included throughout the scenarios, it is important to consider the client's perspective and potential responses given his or her social identity characteristics such as culture, religion, age, sexual orientation, and gender.

Emotional State of the Client

To allow students to demonstrate empathy and respond to emotional cues, actors need to state or demonstrate the emotions associated with this situation. Depending on the level of student learning, the actor's emotional expression should be such that students are able to respond. For example, the mother in a scenario might report being tearful and may cry at times. In scenarios where actors played a client who was upset with services, displays of extreme anger were overwhelming for most students and hence not useful for the OSCE purposes.

Verbatim Items

Word-for-word quotes for the standardized client to use at specific points in the interview are crucial. These prompts ensure that students receive statements or comments that allow demonstration and assessment of the competencies. It is critical that the actor use each prompt every time the role is played, providing a standardized experience for each student. For example, to test cultural competence an actor might be instructed to state, "In my own country this wouldn't be such a problem" and "Tony shouldn't have to take on these responsibilities; he is a boy."

Social Worker's Goals

This section includes the key issues one would expect the student interviewer to explore given the presenting information he or she receives and the information from the client. Standardized clients are told to respond positively if the student explores these key issues.

Instructions for Students

A brief set of instructions to students gives information similar to what a social worker would typically receive in the setting in which the scenario is located. Instructions include the following:

- Information about the service setting
- How clients are referred
- The role of the social worker and focus of the interview
- The number of sessions allowed for each client
- Presenting issues

It is also important to prepare a brief statement for students, which they will read before conducting the OSCE. Students are generally given about 2 or 3 minutes to read this information. The statement provides information typical of that received before an intake interview or from a referral source and should be similar to what a social worker would receive in the setting in which the scenario is located. Information to students includes information about the service setting (e.g., in the case of Mrs. Gonzales, a social worker in an elementary school), how clients access the service or how they are referred (e.g., by a teacher who is concerned with the student's behavior), the role of the social worker and focus of the interview (e.g., to begin to conduct a psychosocial assessment, jointly develop goals, and connect to resources), the number of sessions allowed for each client (e.g., the client might receive an initial visit plus four additional sessions), and presenting issues (e.g., the son's grades are dropping and he has been acting out in class since the father died 6 months earlier).

In pilot testing we found that students were rushing to develop a plan and offer resources during the 15-minute interview. Our goal in teaching was to develop students' competence in building collaborative relationships with clients through all phases of the helping process. Students' interpretations of the performance expectations in the examination context were undermining the essence of what was being taught, however. As a result, in OSCEs we note in bold on the information sheet that this interview is the first 15 minutes of a 60-minute interview. Examples of these statements are found at the beginning of each scenario in Appendix C.

Involve the Standardized Clients in Developing the Case

As noted earlier, if you are able to work with an established standardized patient or client program, this is a useful first step in developing OSCEs. These programs will recruit actors to play the standardized client and work with you to develop and refine the scenario. For programs without access to standardized patient programs, an alternative approach is to recruit actors through Web-based recruitment sites and train them. If the college or university has a drama program, some collaboration can lead to those students being recruited to act as simulated clients, or this might be built into their program as a volunteer experience or as an assignment. In small colleges, however, we strongly caution against using students in the acting department, to eliminate the risk that the actor is known to the student being assessed.

As noted throughout this discussion, a crucial feature of the OSCE is that it is standardized, so any actor playing a simulated client will be required to play the same role many times so that all students in a course are exposed to the same scenario. In multisection courses we have used as many as eight actors to play the same standardized client. All actors are trained together using the same material. Ensuring that there is only minor variation in the way the role is played is the key to preserving the standardized nature of the examination. During the training the actors practice the role with a social worker or faculty member acting as the student. Actors often raise important questions about missing case information that they need to respond to the questions posed by the interviewer. Their feedback and expertise are then incorporated into the case. Also, actors who have worked with the standardized patient program and health profession students can also draw on their past experiences and help you identify areas students might find difficult.

It is apparent that simulation with standardized actors is very different from student role plays. In fact, the actors must bring a professional stance to the scenario so that they are not flooded with the associated emotions that may arise in playing very difficult situations repetitively. Even with their professional training, many standardized patients find a short period of debriefing after playing a client numerous times in one day very useful. In highly emotional case scenarios, debriefing is strongly recommended because actors may have experienced a similar situation in their own lives, triggering their own emotional response. Because playing the same scenario over and over can be tiring, to prevent fatigue and maintain standard case presentation, it is important to give the actors breaks. We have found that actors can play the role approximately six to eight times in a day. Segments are approximately 15 minutes in length, and a scheduled break is provided after three or four performances. When actors play the role during an entire day, a scheduled 1-hour break for lunch is important.

When training the standardized client, begin by orienting the actor to the purpose and format of the activity or examination. Review the basic information about the case and the background information with the actor. As you discuss the role with actors, they are likely to ask for more details and help you clarify points; for example, they may want to know the composition of their nuclear families, age and names of parents and siblings, neighborhood they live in, name of employer, and so forth. A useful technique is to encourage them to draw on information in their own lives or in similar characters they have played in professional productions, and work together to develop these details. When the actors draw on their own frame of reference, they are often able to play the character in a more authentic manner. For example, in the Mrs. Gonzales scenario the standardized client came from Mexico and reflected on changes she had seen in the help one could count on from extended family both in her country of origin and in Canada and how times had changed. Depending on the actor's personal and professional experience, she or he can provide emotional insights to make the case more realistic, which can assist you in fleshing out aspects of the scenario. On the other hand, actors may use their own style to portray the client and the client's reaction to the situation. If this style is not what you want portrayed in the scenario, it is important to clarify that before you enter into field testing. For example, an actor playing a young woman who was questioning her sexual orientation initially played the client as resistant and not forthcoming, not providing students with the information they needed to demonstrate competence in responding to concerns about sexual orientation. The actor was redirected to portray her questioning and confusion in a fairly open manner, as she had sought out the social worker.

As stated previously, it is very important to develop standardized prompts, which the standardized client will offer at specific points through the interview. Often these prompts can be revised through field testing with the actor. In this way the prompts are congruent with the actor's natural ways of expression, adding more authenticity to the portrayal.

It is important to orient the actors to the purpose of the interview, especially in relation to some of the competencies we are aiming to assess. For example, if we want to assess students' ability to use basic interviewing skills in conducting an assessment, we ask the actor not to reveal the entire situation that brings them to the social worker. The actor is asked to intersperse the enactment with brief silences so that students can use skills such as open-ended questions, paraphrase, and exploring implied or underlying thoughts and feelings. Also, we ask the actor to provide some nonverbal, as well as verbal, indications of distress. Verbatim comments might include, "It's so complicated, I don't know where to begin" or "This is hard to talk about."

It has also been helpful to give the actor a sense of the type of responses you have been teaching and expect from students and ask the actor to respond positively to these responses. For example, in a scenario in specialized practice with families, an actor was depicting an upset father in a high-conflict divorce and custody battle. In response to the student's validating comments about the client's experience, the actor was able to become more contained and calm. In contrast, when students ignored the client's emotional state, were passive, or asked multiple questions, the actor continued to demonstrate his anger when responding to the student. Actors are encouraged to consider their natural response to a student's interviewing and relational style to portray how a client might respond in a real situation. Although the scenario is standard, the emotional response of the actor is influenced by the presentation and competence of the student. This allows authenticity in the exam setting.

Props and other cues can also enhance the realism of the scenario and client. For example, in a scenario of an older adult, a walker can be used to emphasize the client's physical frailty. For a scenario with a young, isolated new mother whose baby cries a great deal, the situation can be made more lifelike with a mannequin of a baby that can be programmed to emit sounds such as crying or laughing at specific times in the interview.

Pilot Test the Case Scenario

After one session of training with the actor, it is useful to conduct an initial field test with student volunteers at different points in the program and with experienced social workers. We recommend video recording and reviewing these interviews to determine whether the case scenario, verbatim statements, and actor's portrayal provides enough opportunities for students to work with and demonstrate the competencies being assessed and whether the scenario discriminates between student performance at various points in the educational program and in comparison to experienced social workers. Useful questions to clarify the focus of the OSCE are "What is the issue in the case we want the student to address?" and "What should the student be able to do to address it?" These questions assist in further defining the issues and expected competencies and practice behaviors expected of the students, specifying and describing indicators at points along the rating scale, modifying the scenarios, and providing the actors with additional or revised verbatim statements to use in the interview if the student does not pick up on salient issues. Some examples will highlight these challenges.

One of the goals of the first scenario was to assess students' ability to respond to cultural information and engage with diversity. The scenario involved a Mexican woman who had moved to this country 2 years ago. The simulated client was Mexican and spoke with an accent. Despite these cues, after two pilot tests we observed that student volunteers were not inquiring further about this information, and as a result there was no data to assess cultural competence. It was not clear why this was so, whether students were not aware of the importance of ethnicity, not interested in exploring it, or uncomfortable with difference. In the reflective dialogue in the pilot test the students noted that they were aware of her ethnicity and recent immigration but did not want to appear to the client to be making assumptions based on her appearance. The following verbatim statements were added: "In my own country this wouldn't be such a problem" and "Tony shouldn't have to take on these responsibilities; he is a boy" to provide cultural cues that students in subsequent interviews either responded to, explored with greater or lesser interest, or ignored.

As noted earlier, it is useful to give actors a general sense of the type of student responses expected. In the pilot test this sense can be refined as the actor gains experience in interacting with social workers. For example, the social work model of relationship building taught in the program emphasizes the importance of cogent, supportive comments that reflect feelings and convey empathy. Although this was discussed in the training, in the pilot test we could intervene when the actor who was playing the role did not respond positively when such statements were made but rather ignored them and continued with her agenda. Furthermore, the pilot test can reveal that the actors themselves may demonstrate personal biases that alter how they present the case scenario. For example, an actor with a gender bias may play a role one way with male students and another way with female students, or an actor might convey racist attitudes with students of color. It is important to observe and intervene in these situations to help the actor play the role consistently each time.

To determine whether scenarios were appropriately complex, the scenarios were tested with student volunteers from both years of the MSW program and with experienced practitioners. Each pilot test enabled the team to clarify the specific competency, as expressed on the rating scale, and the way it would be evident in the specific issues to be addressed in each case. Descriptions of practice behaviors at different levels of performance along the rating scale were based on observing these participants.

Whereas some practice behaviors that are assessed on the rating scale are similar across the diverse scenarios (i.e., introducing oneself to the client, collaborating in goal setting), others highlight issues unique to each case, and in some situations they are population specific. For example, gender, culture, and sexual orientation play out differently in each case and raise different issues about cultural competence. The social location of the student interviewee may also influence student responses to the client's issue. Regarding the ability to conduct an ecosystemic assessment, there are both generic and specific relevant issues and resources based on the particular scenario. One dimension of developing a collaborative relationship is addressing feelings, and each case raises an issue of emotional or physical distress (e.g., bereavement, financial concern, conflict with religion). Feedback from the student and practitioner volunteers helped us to examine and discuss these and other issues so that the case and associated rating scale could be revised as needed.

These examples of issues and potential solutions are based on our collective experiences in designing OSCEs largely to assess foundation-level or generalist practice. More recently we have launched projects geared at advanced-level, specialized practice. In these projects, although we found that the expression of competence and practice behaviors need specification and indicators related to the particular learning outcomes desired, the general steps and issues in design were the same as those presented here.

Constructing Measures: Development of the Performance Rating Scale

The OSCE used in medical education generally has the standardized patient complete a binary (yes/no) checklist and serve as a reporter of what the student did. A faculty member, often a clinical instructor, serves as an evaluator and examines the report from the standardized patient to provide a grade for the medical student. In our previous research we found that when field instructors were asked to rate discrete items, it contributed to a deconstructed and reductionist view of competence and distanced them from their holistic impression and evaluation of students (Regehr et al., 2007). Therefore, we aimed to develop a rating scale that would focus assessors on a level of performance that was not so specific and was closer to a global sense of the student's competence on particular dimensions and on the interview as a whole.

The scale we developed (see Appendix B; Bogo et al., 2012) was designed to capture both content and process components of the competencies. This decision is consistent with others' recommendations. For example, Hodges and colleagues (2002) developed OSCEs to assess students on psychiatry rotations and propose that "heavy weight should be given to global ratings that are better able to capture the complex interpersonal interactions emphasized in psychiatry. Qualities such as empathy, organization, and rapport are not well captured by binary checklists" (p. 146). Others recommend rating scales that evaluate specific competencies relevant to the scenarios as well as more global measures of performance (Regehr, MacRae, Reznick, & Szalay, 1998). Following this advice, we included an item from the rating scale (Figure 3) because it provides a global rating of the student's performance. We recommend that any scale developed should include a similar global rating item. In field testing it was found that although raters may differ somewhat in their perception of specific practice behaviors, there was greater agreement in their overall impression of student performance.

As noted earlier, it is important to begin scale construction having identified the competencies and related practice behaviors to be measured. When we are faced with assessing the student's level of performance during pilot testing, these practice behaviors will then be further defined to differentiate between behaviors at the low, middle, or high end of performance. Thus, conceptual and definitional work takes place at three levels: competence, practice behaviors, and a range of performance indicators related to each practice behavior. The items in Figure 4 (from the OSCE for Social Work: Practice Performance Rating Scale) provide an example of these various levels on the scale.

Overall Assessment of the Knowledge and Skills Demonstrated in the Interview				
Based on your impression of the candidate's performance, this candidate demonstrated competence at the level of				
1	2	3	4	5
No initiative or response to components of relationship building and assessment, no organization or cohesion	Very beginning and inconsistent attempts to take initiative, assess and build relationship, inconsistent organization and cohesion	Some consistent initiative and response to some components of relationship building and assessment, consistent organization and cohesion	Usually consistent in response to most components of relationship building and assessment, integrated organization and cohesion	Effective, consistent, perceptive initiative to all components of relationship building and assessment, efficient organization and cohesion

Figure 3. Global rating item.

To review, our scale presented here was designed to measure the following components of competence: develops and uses a collaborative relationship, conducts an ecosystemic assessment, sets the stage for collaborative goal setting, and demonstrates cultural competence. Most of these competencies were further specified as practice behaviors; for example, the competency "Develops and uses a collaborative relationship" was further defined as practice behaviors consisting of (a) introduction; (b) response to client, general content, and process; (c) response to client, specific to situation; and (d) focus of interview. The competency "Conducts an ecosystemic assessment" was further defined as practice behaviors consisting of (a) identifies presenting problem, (b) conducts systemic assessment, and (c) attends to strengths. For the remaining competencies, "Sets the stage for collaborative goal setting" and "Demonstrates cultural competence," only one item serves as the practice behavior.

I. Develops and uses a collaborative relationship				
Introduction				
1	2	3	4	5
Does not introduce self, role, or agency service	Introduces self; no description of role or agency service	Before end of the interview introduces self and role but is general or vague about agency's service	Before end of the interview introduces self, role, and agency service	Sets the stage by introducing self, role in context of agency's service
Response to client: general content and process (about communications and feelings)				
1	2	3	4	5
Inappropriate or no response to client's communications and feelings	Responds to client with cognitive, behavioral, or factual comments; no response to feelings expressed or implied	Mainly task and event focused with occasional warm and empathic response to client's feelings	Frequent warm and empathic responses to client's concerns, expressed and implied feelings	Consistent warm and empathic responses to client's concerns, expressed and implied feelings; assists clients in putting feelings into words

Figure 4. Rating scale items.

Readers can review this rating scale and will note that each competency or practice behavior is then defined at five levels of performance with performance indicators. Originally we worked with a 3-point scale, but in field testing we found it did not differentiate well between students at different levels of education and experienced practitioners. Ultimately, we chose to use a 5-point scale because the latter provided more finely tuned descriptors, which resulted in more differentiation between skill levels. Identification and definitions of levels were continually refined in pilot testing where students and experienced practitioners were observed in simulated interviews. This helped us clarify the dimensions of expected behavior in the interview. The major challenge is to provide enough specificity in defining performance along the 5 points to differentiate between levels of performance. For example, in an early version of the scale all interviewees were ultimately "able to identify the presenting problem and precipitating event" and hence received a rating of 5. However, when we observed the interviews it was obvious that there was great variation in the way the participants went about enacting this behavior. We subsequently defined the item so that a rating of 5 was defined as follows: "Efficiently identifies presenting problem, situation, and precipitant, with linkages between them." This definition differentiates the behavior from a rating of 4, which was defined as follows: "After some time identifies presenting problem, precipitant event, and situation."

Much energy went into defining each level in detail so that we had increasingly clear behavioral descriptors of the component being assessed. However, we conclude that although it is useful to provide descriptions of behavioral indicators, efforts at exact definitions can involve the team in endless work that may not be necessary. In our earlier research on competence evaluation in field education, we found that field instructors form a general impression of a student's performance, and this influences their ratings. In training raters for the OSCE, many read these fine-tuned descriptors very carefully. However, we are not certain that when in the actual OSCE situation the raters attended as much to these definitions. It is useful to remember that designing an OSCE is an iterative process. As you use the scale, whether in a pilot or for actual assessment, you will continue to refine your indicators and case scenarios.

Initially, we tried to provide a label for each of the five levels in the rating scale, experimenting with terms such as poor, not ready to practice, needs more training, good, average, competent, excellent, and exemplary. This further complicated the work of defining and achieving enough uniformity in interpretation of these labels for each of the competencies and practice behaviors. At one point labels were used only on the overall assessment item: 1 (inferior), 2 (poor), 3 (needs more training), 4 (good), and 5 (excellent). The final scale has no labels and only uses numbers 1 to 5, because the raters, who are the course instructors, found that the negative nature of some of the labels interfered with their ability to score a 1 or 2 rating. This was consistent with our earlier findings about social work field instructors' experiences in evaluating students; they did not like to label or categorize students negatively (Bogo et al., 2007). The merits of using labels to define the rating level are debatable, and further empirical work is needed. We recommend that when designing a scale, you consider what the benchmark for performance is for the level of student being assessed. For example, at what level would you expect a first-year student to be able to perform? Similarly, what is the expected level for a second-year student? These considerations can help you develop the performance indicators for the various ratings.

To provide a focus for the raters who are assessing student performance, a list of basic interviewing behaviors based on Bogo (2006) was developed. This list helped orient the raters to aspects of the interview to be attended to. These interviewing behaviors included appropriate use of open- and closed-ended questions; seeking clarification and concreteness; restatement or paraphrase of content, thoughts, and meanings; reflecting feelings; appropriate use of silence; and providing a summary. Two dimensions of active listening were included: nonverbal behaviors (e.g., appropriate body posture, facial expression, encouragement such as head nods, attentive gaze) and verbal behaviors (e.g., voice tone, speech, volume). These behaviors are not assessed because the researchers chose not to focus on micro skills but rather on the way the student integrated these skills to demonstrate procedural competence, or complex practice behaviors, to engage in a relationship, conduct an assessment, attend to culture, and so on. This decision is consistent with the conceptualization of holistic competence as discussed in Chapter 1 and presented in Figure 1. As previously described, consistent with research on global measures, one global item is assessed (Regehr et al., 1998), in this case the knowledge and skills demonstrated in the interview.

The rating scale was developed to use with a range of scenarios that one would expect a student could engage with at the end of the first semester or first year in an MSW or BSW program. If instructors are designing a multistation OSCE in which the student is being rated on several different scenarios, the same rating scale for all scenarios is recommended to reflect interstation reliability for each student. Items on the rating scale must be defined at a general enough level to be relevant to all scenarios. To cue the rater to specifics for each scenario, the rating scale includes the content or topic in each dimension. For example, for the dimension "Response to Client: Specific to Situation" we added in brackets "about death of husband, illness, accident, coming out youth, elderly, child protection" specific to each case. These labels are related to the first five scenarios in Appendix C.

As noted throughout this book, the development of the OSCE is an iterative process going back and forth from conceptualizing and defining what one wants to measure, ensuring the scenario provides the material students can respond to, and actually using the scale to rate performance to determine whether the scale captures the dimensions the rater is interested in assessing. The process of testing and retesting the scale should involve not only those who created the scale but also instructors or raters who will ultimately use the scale. A useful testing format is to have instructors and potential raters rate video-recorded interviews of the scenarios conducted during pilot work, compare their ratings on each item, and discuss their rationale for the rating.

Instructors can design their own scales following the suggestions provided or use or modify the scales provided in Appendix B to correspond to the competencies and practice behaviors they chose to assess using an OSCE. For example, a practice behavior related to the competence of risk assessment was developed for use with a case scenario involving suicide risk. (See Appendix B, Supplemental Risk Assessment Scale Item.) The method lends itself to assessing additional competencies, and as more social work educators design and test the approach, it is likely that a wide range of tools will be available for teaching, assessment, and research. It is hoped that other teams will benefit from the experience and steps described and that they will use these strategies to develop additional scales and related case scenarios.

Developing the Reflection Component of the OSCE and the Reflection Rating Scale

As discussed at the beginning of this chapter, the first step in designing an OSCE is to identify competencies and associated practice behaviors. Some components that inform the demonstration and assessment of practice behaviors are not directly observable, such as the cognitive and subjective processes involved in using knowledge, values, reflecting on judgment, self-awareness, and self-regulation. The Toronto team was especially interested in assessing three components based on the conceptualization of holistic competence: conceptualization of practice (content and process) including engaging diversity, self-regulation (affective and cognitive), and professional development (learning and growth) (Bogo, Regehr, Logie, et al., 2011). They chose a reflective activity for this purpose. For instructors who design an OSCE following EPAS (CSWE, 2014), a review of the descriptions of the interrelated components of each competency can guide decisions about whether to use a reflective activity and which components of the competency to include. Specific components of each competency can be elaborated to assess key aspects that are relevant to the course, to generalist or specialized practice, to the purpose of the assessment, and to the issues portrayed in the scenario.

Questions and probes for a postinterview reflective dialogue were developed following the procedures of Barrows (2000b) for stimulated recall and include questions designed to elicit information that would enable us to assess these dimensions. The goal was to use the performance in the interview as a spring-board and focus for reflection. Although there is extensive discussion about reflective practice in the literature, we found no reports of structured reflection on a specific observed performance, conducted immediately after an interview. An initial set of questions was developed, field tested with social work students and practitioners, and continuously revised and refined until we were able to arrive at questions that elicited textured reflections in a meaningful order. Initially the questions were posed by the rater immediately after the student interview with the client. The rater created the atmosphere of an interactive dialogue rather than an examination-like stance with a correct answer. When the OSCE plus reflection was administered to the entire student body of 150, given limited time and resources, the dialogue was replaced with students proceeding to a computer lab immediately after their live interview with the actor and writing responses to the questions on a computer. These written responses were then submitted to the rater who had recently observed the interview. Responses were then rated using the Reflection Rating Scale (see Appendix B, "Reflection Questions After the Interview" and "OSCE for Social Work: Post-OSCE Reflection Rating Scale").

As we have described elsewhere, we developed and tested the Reflection Scale in the following manner (Bogo, Regehr, Katz, et al., 2011). In a series of pilot tests, students at various levels in the program and experienced social workers conducted an OSCE interview and then participated in a reflective dialogue:

All reflective dialogues were digitally recorded, transcribed, and analyzed to identify the continuum of responses. Through thematic analysis of the transcripts three descriptors along a five-point rating scale for each sub-category were identified. Subsequent pilot testing and analysis resulted in three drafts of the questions/probes and three drafts of the reflection scale. (p. 189)

We offer the following observation for others interested in developing a reflective component to the OSCE. We learned very early the importance of designing questions carefully to get rich responses that reflected student cognitive and affective processes. For example, what we asked for is what we received. That is, when we asked students to "Identify values of social work that you were using during your interaction with the client," they talked about nonjudgmental attitude and self-determination. When we changed this to "Identify principles of social work that you were using during your interaction with the client," they talked about starting where the client is and going at the client's pace. We then tried to ask about "ideas from social work" and ultimately phrased it, "Can you think of something that you have learned from social work that influenced your approach during this interview?" This question resulted in a wide range of responses and included how students used explanatory theories, practice theories, values, notions about self, and/or interviewing skills (Bogo et al., 2013). Similar to the performance rating scale, it is imperative that you pilot test the reflection rating scale using the reflective responses to determine whether the reflective questions are eliciting the information needed and whether the scale is able to identify gradations in responses.

Conceptualizing Diversity for an OSCE

Social work educators are committed to ensuring that graduates are competent in engaging and working respectfully and effectively with diversity and difference in practice, as evident throughout EPAS (CSWE, 2014). In an attempt to clarify and operationalize components of cultural competence, Kwong (2012) notes there are challenges for assessment and suggests the use of standardized clients as one possibility. We concur with this recommendation, as illustrated by the examples in this chapter that demonstrate how competency in practice with diversity, difference, and culture can be conceptualized and included in designing an OSCE. This section reviews social work education literature and research particularly addressing this issue and relevant information from related health professions.

OSCE lends itself well to assessing students' competence in engaging diversity and difference as an integrated part of practice. As noted in Chapter 1, Lu and colleagues (2011) developed and established psychometric properties of a rating scale to assess students' clinical practice competence that included cultural sensitivity. These authors describe the process of identifying and specifying indicators related to cultural sensitivity, which include demonstration of "awareness of their own culture, sensitivity to diverse cultural values and constructs, and proficiency in cross-cultural communication" (p. 174). For this study, six standardized client situations were constructed with diversity related to age, gender, race, religion, sexual orientation, and socioeconomic status. The rating scale for this study can be found in Lu and colleagues (2011, p. 175).

Similarly, in our initial study we were interested in assessing students' competence in working with intersecting diversities (Bogo, Regehr, Logie, et al., 2011). We conceptualized this competency as including the way in which students perform in relation to the cultural cues and content presented explicitly and implicitly by clients, and students' ability to use concepts related to the effect of social identity factors on clients' experiences and interpretations of their situation, with the associated implications for practice. When we designed the conceptual map to guide the project, intersecting diversity factors were included in all scenarios, as described in Table 2. Culture, class and ethnicity, gender, sexual orientation, and age were dimensions incorporated in all case scenarios (see Appendix C, "Case Scenarios"). In an iterative fashion, through pilot testing and construction of the assessment measure, the competency was defined more specifically. One item on the Performance Rating Scale titled "Demonstrates cultural competence related to culture/gender/race/sexual orientation/age-ability" is used for assessment (see Appendix B). Indicators on the 5-point scale relate to degree of comfort, recognition, interest, and ability in exploring cultural cues and differences to understand the client and demonstrating an appreciation of the client's cultural identity.

During the pilot phase we observed that students and practitioners varied in the degree to which they demonstrated competence in the interview, but in the postinterview reflection many were aware of the effects of diversity issues on the client and varied in their ability to integrate and use their insights in practice. Accordingly, both a reflective question and an item on the reflection rating scale were further refined to assess this component of competence (see Appendix B).

In a subsequent analysis of students' responses demonstrating their understanding and engagement with diversity in the interview, three patterns emerged (Bogo et al., 2013). First, one group of students integrated their understanding and past practicum experiences of working with cultural differences and with immigrant clients into their performance in the simulated interviews. Their responses were thoughtful, including insights into the effects of discrimination, language barriers, specific culturally based values, lack of networks, and the perception of similarities and differences between the client and student. A second group of students recognized the effect of diversity and used the term, but to identify numerous reasons why they did not explicitly address related issues in the interview. This included a perception that doing so would make the client uncomfortable, that they had learned to avoid labeling clients, that all clients should be treated in the same way, and that they lacked the skill to demonstrate cultural sensitivity. The latter observation was particularly evident in analyses of students' reflections with a simulated client who was coming out as lesbian and was convinced that her family's cultural and religious background would be intolerant (Logie, Bogo, & Katz, in press). Some students identified their lack of knowledge and appropriate terminology to speak respectfully with this client, and many highlighted the need for skills training; they "felt not 'equipped' to work on sexual orientation issues" (Logie et al., in press, p. 13). Also, students experienced challenges in managing their personal reactions to the client's unexpected disclosure of same-sex attraction. Returning to the analysis of students' reflections on all the scenarios, a third group of students were those who minimized or ignored diversity factors that were obvious, such as racial identity, struggles related to immigration status, and age differences (Bogo et al., 2013).

These studies conducted with social work students demonstrate that the OSCE method is highly effective for assessing students' competency in engaging diversity and difference in practice. The literature in related health professions such as medicine and nursing presents examples of studies that use OSCE to promote positive attitudes and some skill development in working cross-culturally. Surprisingly, only a few studies use OSCE to assess student learning and performance of this crucial competency. For example, in nursing education there is a commitment to support care for all patients by enhancing knowledge and skills for practice with culturally diverse clients. In one study, the researchers based their innovation on work previously done in nursing and related health professions and provided a knowledge-based module followed by a two-station OSCE (Ndiwane, Omanand, & Theroux, 2014). Scales administered before and after the module examined knowledge, attitudes, and satisfaction. Ratings of student performance by the standardized patients were positive, and students reviewed their video-recorded interviews and reported that their critical thinking skills improved. However, assessment of individual students' performance in the OSCE was not provided by faculty, although general themes were discussed with the student group.

Medical educators have also been writing about the importance of students' developing cultural or intercultural competence, and some have reported using OSCE as a teaching tool, similar to a formative assessment. For example, a workshop followed by a five-station OSCE was used by an interdisciplinary group of health professionals to teach medical residents cultural competence for use in encounters with patients from any culture (Aeder et al., 2007). Rating scales consisting of two components, communication and cultural skills, were designed for use in debriefing and gaining feedback from standardized clients, faculty observers, and participants. Evaluation focused on residents' satisfaction with the method for improving their competence, but OSCE was not used to formally assess their performance. Satisfaction with the teaching method was high, and face validity was established in this project.

In a similar vein Miller and Green (2007) studied the effects of including a cultural competence station in a set of OSCE scenarios for medical students.

Students perceived that they learned a range of competencies related to exploring patients' culturally based perspectives about their illness, medications, and alternative treatments. The authors conclude that OSCE is a valuable method for teaching about cross-cultural care. In a reflective article, Hamilton (2009) states,

> If we accept that the Objective Structured Clinical Examination (OSCE) is the most appropriate and reliable tool for assessing student communication and clinical skills in intercultural contexts, then the next question is at what stage of a course is it reasonable [to] start assessing this. (p. 862)

Issues related to timing of content in an already overloaded curriculum are discussed, with the author highlighting the necessity of numerous experiential learning opportunities with guided reflection and feedback for students to learn not only specific knowledge but also skills.

This brief discussion of the use of OSCE in educational assessment of competence with respect to diversity appears to indicate that social work educators are well-positioned to provide leadership to health profession colleagues in conceptualizing and assessing competence in this dimension of practice. This is understandable, given the profession's long-standing commitment and attention to social justice, equity, diversity, and cultural competence. As social work instructors increasingly use simulation in teaching and in assessing competency, it is likely that a growing body of evidence-based methods and scales will be available for dissemination.

Summary of Steps for a Social Work OSCE

The steps to be undertaken when creating an OSCE are summarized here in a linear fashion; as noted throughout this chapter, however, a cumulative and iterative process is involved. Working backward and forward through the various phases was crucial in assisting us to more clearly identify and define the components associated with the competencies we aimed to measure and in developing and refining the assessment methods.

Identify Competencies and Associated Practice Behaviors

- Review the accreditation framework (if applicable), the curriculum, and educational objectives and identify the competencies to be assessed.
- Choose particular competencies that can be reasonably assessed in an OSCE, including components of competencies to be assessed in a reflection if the instructor wants to use this method.
- Work backward to identify the substantive content and learning activities needed so that students can master the knowledge, skills, and values associated with the competence. Review the attention paid in teaching and learning to developing competence in cognitive and subjective processes such as critical thinking, awareness and management of subjective reactions, and effects on judgment.
- Review the curriculum or course to ensure that this content is taught to students.

Create a Conceptual Map of Competencies, Issues, and Content

- Working iteratively, consider one or more potential scenarios including central issues and some specific content.
- Link competencies and practice behaviors to issues and content.

Develop the OSCE Case (at the Same Time Construct Measures)

- Draft a case scenario in some detail covering
  - history and background information,
  - emotional state of the client,
  - verbatim statements that allow students to demonstrate the competencies,
  - key issues that students are expected to cover, and
  - instructions for students before conducting the interview.
- Work with an actor to pilot test and further develop the case.
- Pilot test the scenario with students at various levels and experienced practitioners to determine
  - whether the scenario provides enough information for students to demonstrate the competency and practice behaviors and

– clarify what is expected in student performance to address the issues in the scenario.

Construct Measures

- Use the identified competencies, associated practice behaviors, and conceptual map to draft a rating scale. For each item define behavioral indicators for a 5-point scale, including a global measure of performance.
- Pilot test the scale with raters observing students at various levels and experienced practitioners conducting the interview to determine
  – whether items and indicators on the scale capture the range of behaviors and
  – the authenticity of the case.
- Work iteratively to refine the conceptual map, the specific issues to be addressed, the competencies to be observed, the case scenario, and the rating scale.

CHAPTER 3

Preparing and Implementing a Social Work OSCE

In the previous chapters the conceptual and developmental foundations of the OSCE were reviewed and approaches to preparing for OSCE presented. These preparations are pivotal to the success of the OSCE method and, though time-consuming, essential to assessment of the competencies. The next stage involves the practical steps to organize the implementation of the OSCE with students. This chapter provides details about the relevant tasks.

Format of the OSCE

Providing an OSCE involves numerous steps and activities. In this section we provide a template; each step can be modified based on the goals of the exercise and pragmatic considerations, including resources. Video recordings that illustrate the various steps can be accessed at http://youtu.be/vFSd9D6PF18 and http://youtu.be/JMvsgNVBrtk. Each program must carefully consider its unique needs and resources while maintaining the integrity of the exam.

The following format has been used successfully in examining 150 students over 2 days with eight raters. This basic outline has also been used in smaller programs or for programs running only one station at a time. Alternatives are also noted. In the following format the OSCE rater is not the student's course instructor; the rationale for this design is discussed further in this chapter.

Before the OSCE
- One week before the OSCE, provide students with the date, time, and location of their OSCE and the name of the person who will rate their

performance and reflection. Another option is to have students sign up for a specific date and time. Providing the name of the rater is optional.

- Students are told they must arrive on time. Given the number of students to be examined on one day, interviews must start exactly on time. Latecomers are not permitted to complete the exam.

- When students arrive at the site, they check in at a designated room, where they receive three labels. Each label has the student's name, course instructor's name, and the name of the OSCE rater. They are also given the room number where the interview will be conducted. One label is for the Performance Rating Scale, another label is for the Reflection Rating Scale, and the third label is for the student's written Reflection. Another option to identify students is for the rater to simply write the student's name on the various scales.

- Five minutes before the start of the OSCE, students are seated outside the designated room. A bell or buzzer is sounded that alerts students and raters that the examination will begin. Another option is to have a designated faculty facilitator announce to students to begin the exam.

The OSCE

- The rater greets the student who is sitting outside the interview room and provides the student with a half-page written description of the case scenario with information one would find on a brief telephone intake form. Appendix C contains client scenarios, all of which include the intake information and brief instructions about the role of the social worker. Another option is to provide this information to students in their class before the OSCE.

- When the student enters the examination room, she or he gives the rater two labels with the student's name, course instructor's name, and the name of the OSCE rater. The rater places one label on the Performance Rating Scale and one label on the Reflection Rating Scale. If not using labels, as noted earlier, the rater can simply write the student's name on the various scales.

- Students are given 2–3 minutes to read the case scenario. Another option is to allow students to take notes on the intake form as they might in a real situation.

- A bell or buzzer is sounded to signal that students are to enter the interviewing room and begin the interview. Another option is to have a designated faculty facilitator announce that it is time for students to enter the interviewing room.
- Students conduct the interview for approximately 12–15 minutes. (The exact duration of the interview is based on scheduling issues such as how many students will be examined on a particular day.)
- A bell, buzzer, or knock on the door can be used to signal that there are 4 minutes remaining in the interview. This method is optional because some students reported that it was distracting. However, other students reported that it was helpful because it primed them to provide some closure to the interview. Based on your stated competencies, you can decide which method works best for your program. For example, because we structured the OSCE to represent the first 15 minutes of a 45-minute interview, there was no need to signal to students that they should begin to summarize and wrap up the session. Therefore, there is no longer a signal until the interview time is completed.
- A bell or buzzer alerts participants that the interview is over.
- The actor comes out of character and provides brief feedback to the student, followed by feedback from the rater to a maximum of 5 minutes in total. This step is optional, based on whether there will be other opportunities for feedback, for example in class, from colleagues, and from the course instructor. Another option involves the actor preparing brief written feedback while the rater provides verbal feedback. The actor's written feedback will be given to the student after her or his self-reflection.
- The rater takes the brief written description of the case scenario from the student so it can be provided to the next student, who will arrive in approximately 10 minutes.
- While the student is conducting the interview, the rater, who is in the interviewing room and observing the interview between the student and the actor, uses the Performance Rating Scale to rate the student's performance. After the student leaves the room there is approximately 10 minutes for the rater to review the ratings and to write additional

brief notes for use by the course instructor in providing feedback to the student. Raters actually needed only 5 minutes for this step; however, the break provides time for the rater to prepare for the next student.

Reflection Component of the OSCE

As noted earlier, use of a reflection component allows the student and rater to assess important additional components of holistic competence for effective social work practice that are not easily assessed solely through observation of the interview. Although we strongly recommend the use of a reflective component, the process and focus for recall, reflection, and discussion will vary based on the identified outcomes for assessment and the learning goals for the examination. The process described in this chapter is one example of accessing specific components of competence associated with the model of holistic competence in social work presented in Chapter 1, Figure 1, and discussed further in Chapter 2. This conceptualization led to the design of the Reflection Questions and Reflection Rating Scale (Bogo, Regehr, Katz, et al., 2011). Depending on the programs' identification of competencies and practice behaviors for assessment in an OSCE, specific reflection questions can be designed with a corresponding reflection rating scale.

A reflective activity can be carried out in a variety of ways. The following are formats used by our two teams.

Option 1

- After completing the interview and receiving approximately 5 minutes of feedback from the actor and the rater, students proceed to a computer lab. There is a computer for each student, with the reflection questions and space to respond already loaded on each computer. Students have 25 minutes to write their responses to the reflection questions.
- Students then print one copy of their Reflective Responses and place the third student label (which contains the student's name, course instructor's name, and the name of the OSCE rater) on the printed Reflective Responses document and place the Reflective Responses document in a box outside the exam rater's room.

- The OSCE is scheduled so that the rater has time to review and rate the Reflective Responses using the Post-OSCE Reflection Rating Scale. Because the rater has seen the interview and has the Performance Rating Scale and her or his notes, raters are easily able to recall the interview as they read and rate each student's Reflective Responses. Raters will often write notes on the Post-OSCE Reflection Rating Scale, especially when the student's reflections include comments about the student's performance that the rater did not observe. Consistent with the literature on recall and self-assessment, we have observed this phenomenon; students believe and report they behaved in particular ways that actually did not occur.

- The rater then assembles for each student the Performance Rating Scale, the student's Reflective Responses, and the Post-OSCE Reflection Rating Scale. The OSCE coordinator ensures that these documents are given to the student's course instructor.

- In this example, the raters' ratings and written comments on these scales for each student observed are integrated by the course instructor into a written feedback form given to the student (see Appendix D). This form includes details about assessment of competencies and specific practice behaviors, including those that have been demonstrated and those that need further development. Suggestions for learning methods to increase competence are also included, based on the student's performance in the course and in the OSCE (e.g., the need to take more initiative, more opportunity to observe interviews and debrief, strategies for emotional self-regulation to contain performance anxiety). (See Appendix D for specific instructions for students for this assignment, and see Appendix E for a detailed set of instructions for the OSCE rater.)

Option 2

- An alternative approach to accessing components of holistic competence using reflection involves the rater asking the student reflective questions, with the student responding verbally. Although this format provides insight to the rater and student about thoughts and feelings underlying the student's performance, it is more difficult to evaluate than when using a reflection scale with a written document from the student. The verbal responses primarily serve the purpose of raising students' consciousness about the underlying implicit and explicit knowledge, values, and cognitive and subjective processes related to how their own experiences and educational background have informed their performance. When using a verbal interaction it is more difficult to conduct a formal assessment, but this process is still very valuable, especially for students who are early in their educational careers and may still be very focused on task performance. A reflective process helps students think critically about their own use of self in their work with the client.

Option 3

- A useful option to assess additional components of holistic competence involves designing an assignment built on the OSCE. Such an assignment has been used to assess the way in which students integrate their understanding of a range of social work concepts such as self-awareness, gender considerations, and the effects of diversity and difference in practice. Because the OSCE is graded, it serves as an incentive to students to take the exercise seriously and to practice their skills with each other before the exam. In this option the OSCE is video recorded, and the performance rating accounts for 70% of the student's grade. Students are given a copy of the recording and must view their performance and write reflections. Students are given approximately 5–7 days to complete their reflection. They are encouraged to watch their videotape at least three times before writing their paper, because experience has shown that in the first viewing they seem to focus on superficial qualities, the second time they focus on mistakes, and the third time appears to result in a more realistic appraisal. The quality of their reflective responses accounts for 30% of the grade. Each student receives a grade for her or his performance on the exam and on the quality of the reflective responses. (See Appendix D for specific instructions for students for this assignment.)

Option 4

- Similar to the preceding options is a two-part assignment designed to assess competence in a specialized practice course on using mindfulness in social work practice. The assignment is based on a 15-minute OSCE simulated interview held toward the end of the course. The OSCE is video recorded. Immediately after the interview, students write a reflection in response to a set of questions designed to assess students' integration in their interviews of key course concepts. The interview is rated by the instructor, who provides written feedback to the student about his or her performance. The second part of the assignment involves students transcribing and critically reviewing the video recording of their interview. This assignment is submitted 2 weeks after the OSCE. Students transcribe the interview and use a template provided by the instructor that includes identifying specific concepts, competencies, and behavioral indicators. Furthermore, students are expected to provide a rationale for their choice of specific behaviors and critically analyze the effectiveness of their action or, whether on reflection, they would take different actions. (See Appendix D for specific instructions for students enrolled in a course on mindfulness therapy.)

Debriefing the OSCE and Bridging to the Field Practicum

Students have reported significant learning that occurs simply from participating in an OSCE. Also, if one class meeting is held after the OSCE, the course instructor can further reinforce the learning, linking the insights gained from the OSCE with the key course concepts, competencies, practice behaviors, and skills. A successful method involves the course instructor summarizing her or his observations of performance on the OSCE and presenting this information to the class as a whole, without revealing identifying information. We have found that often there are themes that are pervasive across the group of students. For example, in the case example of Mrs. Gonzalez, students often struggle with addressing issues of grief and loss, and they move quickly to resource provision. With the case of Natalya Petrovich, students generally validate and normalize the young mother's feeling of being overwhelmed with a new baby but do not explore potential child neglect. Exploring themes such as these can generate learning for the class beyond the individual experience. It is also helpful in the debrief to explore such areas as students' subjective reactions, strategies they used for managing their anxiety, areas they felt well-prepared for in the interview, and areas in which they believe they need more preparation. It is also helpful to get feedback on their experience of the process and to solicit suggestions on how the process may be improved the next year.

Student performance on the OSCE can provide data useful for informing competence and skill development in the field practicum. Student performance on the OSCE can indicate areas for both students and field instructors to be aware of and work on as part of further development. It can also identify strong students who may be better suited for field settings where a higher level of skill development can occur. There are multiple ways to use the data to help students to bridge learning from courses to the field. Here are some examples.

- OSCE has been used in a delayed-entry program in the first term of a graduate social work program. Students enter the field after completing the first term. When students begin the practicum, they must provide the field instructor with the Final Feedback Form for the Social Work Practice Laboratory Course. (See Appendix D.) The field instructor is expected to use the information provided to begin to develop the learning plan and contract for the field.

- The faculty field liaison receives the learning contract and reviews it in relation to the lab evaluation to ensure that key areas identified for attention will be addressed in the field practicum. In this way, there is a purposeful method to bridge and integrate class and field learning and performance and to build on the knowledge gained in the school about the student's developing competence.

- Another variation on linking class and field can occur in pre–field placement interviews with the field coordinator or faculty field liaison asking the student to report on her or his OSCE experience and feedback received from raters. Based on that information, they can explore possible choices and focus for the upcoming field placement.

Preparing the OSCE Site

In universities where there is a simulation center, often found in medical schools or health professions programs, social work educators may be able to negotiate use of such facilities at little or no cost. Schools without a medical school may have behavioral research labs available for use. Such facilities are usually equipped with video cameras and microphones. New software in many simulation labs allows students and instructors to access video recordings remotely. If video recording is available, each student can then receive a DVD or have access to the recording for use in further learning and assessment activities. Such educational activities can include other students or the instructor reviewing the interview and offering feedback.

Where a simulation center is not available, teaching faculty can use their own offices, or classrooms can easily be set up to provide an interviewing area. For the OSCE run by the Toronto team, a chair is placed outside the faculty office or outside a classroom where students will sit in preparation for the examination. The standardized client has already been seated in the room. The rater sits to one side; she or he can be behind a desk. The rater attempts to be as unobtrusive as possible but should be seated where it is easy to observe the nonverbal reactions of the student and the interaction between the student and client as much as possible. If a video or audio recorder is used, it should be placed in the room and tested before the OSCE. Although video recordings are useful for student and instructor review, we do not recommend that video recordings be used instead of a live rater. We have found that being in the room with the student allows for the most authentic experience of the student's verbal and nonverbal interactions with the standardized client.

In setting up the OSCE, it is also helpful to have a break room for the actors. As previously stated, they can experience fatigue playing the role multiple times. It is important to monitor their level of fatigue and emotional response to the experience so that a standardized presentation of the scenario is maintained. Refreshments available through the day are also appreciated. Break times and lunch for the actors must be included in scheduling.

Recruiting and Training Examiners

When planning the use of an OSCE, consideration should be given to the most appropriate personnel to use as examiners and raters. In developing the OSCE we recruited and trained experienced field instructors, course instructors, and doctoral students with practice backgrounds. Research has identified a leniency bias that occurs when the rater and student have a relationship (Bogo et al., 2007; Vinton & Wilke, 2011), so one option is to arrange the OSCE so that students are not rated by their own course instructor. This can be done in multisection courses with all students randomly assigned to one of the course section instructors, all of whom have been trained together to administer the scales. In small schools where there may be only one instructor for the course, field instructors, local practitioners, or other faculty have been used, with the instructor acting as the administrator of the exam (i.e., keeping track of time, running the video equipment, and attending to all logistics). Raters who have experience in working with students are recommended because they appear to have a better understanding of reasonable expected performance levels.

When course instructors are raters, training on assessment flows naturally from their participation in designing the course objectives, competencies expected, and teaching activities to reach these goals, including using standardized simulations. Therefore, training can focus on achieving enough agreement on the interpretation of the various descriptors and points on the rating scale. A useful process begins with a brief review of the competencies to be measured as described on the rating scale. Instructors can then watch a 10-minute segment of a student interview with a standardized client similar to the one they will be rating in the OSCE. Such interviews can be developed with student volunteers or doctoral students, with consent obtained to use for training purposes. While watching the scenario, instructors rate the student's performance. After making their independent ratings, taking each item at a time, each instructor reports his or her rating. Where there is commonality in ratings, this is noted; where there is discrepancy, instructors discuss their reasons for the rating chosen, examining differences until there is some common understanding of the meaning of all items on the scale.

We strongly recommend that at least two scenarios be used in the training. This activity takes approximately 3 hours. Based on our experience training instructors, we found that the first time instructors rated a student interview, they had numerous questions and some confusion. After discussing the issues, they rated a second student performance in another scenario and achieved much better agreement, more quickly, arriving at more common interpretation of good to poor performance.

The same process is used to train raters to rate the reflection component of the OSCE using the Reflection Rating Scale. A written reflection completed by the same student who conducted the simulated interview is provided to the instructors. After their independent ratings, they share their individual ratings and discuss their rationale.

In our study of 125 MSW students' performance on an OSCE at the end of their first-semester courses, instructors served as raters (Bogo et al., 2012). No significant differences in scores between individual raters were found on the OSCE Performance Rating Scale. On the OSCE Reflection Rating Scale, two raters were significantly different from the others, with one rater having significantly lower scores and one rater having significantly higher scores. These findings were then used for training these instructors as raters in the subsequent year, with the instructors achieving much greater consistency in ratings.

When raters who are not course instructors are used, more time is needed for training. Raters must be oriented to the goals and purpose of the course or program and the competencies to be tested in the OSCE before participating in the rating. Subsequently, the method described earlier has proved sufficient in training. In contrast, we have observed colleagues conducting OSCEs in family medicine and psychiatry. Clinical instructors are invited to serve as examiners of medical students who have completed their rotation in the respective specialties. Orientation was brief, consisting of discussion of forms and logistics of the exam. The expectation was that the community of raters had a common conceptualization of the competencies expected of the students at the specific level of education and could assess the students they would observe without the need for extensive discussion.

Some common pitfalls we discovered through the process used to train raters are described here. Throughout implementation of the OSCE, it is important to have a faculty coordinator who can observe and provide feedback to the raters immediately.

Negative Reactions

Some field instructors or experienced social workers had strong reactions to poor performances by students on the video recordings used in the training. These reactions related to students' verbal or nonverbal behaviors, which these raters perceived reflected qualities not appropriate for social workers; generally they reacted to the students' lack of response to clients' emotions. In some instances these reactions were connected to these instructors' opinions about the weaknesses of social work education, for example, that it is not sufficiently practice focused. These attitudes affected these raters when they assessed students' performance, producing lower scores in many instances. Of equal concern was the observation that when these raters expressed their strong negative reactions to the student's performance it affected the general group discussion, skewing it in a more critical direction. This discussion may also have affected the subsequent ratings by the participating raters when they rated student performance in the second student interview.

In selecting raters we attempt to find people who understand the context of the social work education program and have reasonable expectations of students' performance. However, when highly negative and harsh opinions are expressed by some participants, faculty trainers need to contain these sentiments, pointing out students' developmental levels and the range of acceptable student behavior. Negativity can affect the atmosphere in the training group and hence others' ratings.

Overly Positive Reactions

Similarly, some raters tend to rate more highly than others, producing inflated scores for students. This tendency is recognized throughout social work education literature and especially in field education (Bogo, 2010; Sowbel, 2011; Vinton & Wilke, 2011), and as noted earlier it was found in the case of some ratings on the Reflection Rating Scale in our study (Bogo et al., 2012). In training sessions this tendency can be discussed, but it is useful to note that achieving enough interrater reliability will probably remain an ongoing issue in rating social work competency, where a degree of subjective judgment will always be present.

Finally, it has been useful to provide raters with a very detailed list of instructions and to briefly review this list with them before the actual OSCE. Once raters have participated in one or two OSCE interviews and ratings, they will probably not need to refer to this list again. (See Instructions for OSCE Raters in Appendix E.)

After the OSCE

After the OSCE is completed, it is important to schedule a brief time for raters and instructors to debrief the experience. Useful information for improving the experience can be gained from discussion immediately after the event to note trends in student performance. As noted in Chapter 2, it is also useful to spend time with the actors to debrief their experience.

Tasks

Based on Hodges et al.'s (2002) checklist of tasks for a standardized examination, supplemented with our respective experiences, Table 3 outlines the tasks to be completed for a social work OSCE and the timeframe in which to complete the tasks.

OSCE Forms

As described earlier, there are specific forms for the participants and examiners that can be modified for use. These include the following and can be found in the related appendices.

- Case Scenario for students and for actors (Appendix C)
- Performance Rating Scale (Appendix B)
- Reflection Questions After the Interview, loaded on computers, with copies for raters to use in rating (Appendix B)

- Post-OSCE Reflection Rating Scale (Appendix B)
- Interview Schedule (Appendix E)
- Instructions for OSCE Raters (Appendix E)

In Appendix D we include assignments and forms that have been used with the OSCE at Azusa Pacific University and at the University of Toronto.

Table 3. Planning the Social Work OSCE	
Timeframe	Task
At least 4 months ahead	Ensure that all instructors are involved in planning for the OSCE.
	Draft the standardized client scenario and role or select an existing scenario (see Appendix C).
	Hire an OSCE coordinator to assist with the process or select an instructor to coordinate, providing workload credit as indicated for size of project.
	Hire the standardized client trainer who recruits and trains actors or, if doing this on your own, begin to recruit actors.
	Book the location for the OSCE.
	If conducting research on the OSCE, prepare and submit the ethics protocol.
	Develop a process for monitoring and improving the OSCE.
	Begin to prepare all materials for the OSCE.
	Coordinate the timeframe for the OSCE with the standardized client and examiners, taking into consideration issues such as student exams and holidays.
	If using a computer-based reflection assignment, ensure that computers are available and students can access printing.
6 weeks ahead	Locate, purchase, or rent needed equipment to record the OSCE (DVDs, video camera, audio recorder for backup).
	Do a mock run-through of an OSCE to fine tune scheduling and discover any problems to be addressed.
1 month ahead	Confirm schedule with course instructors and raters.
	Set up a clear schedule with exact times for the person who will send the signal to start and end, using a bell or buzzer.
	Schedule examinations so that students are not matched with their course instructors and each rater has approximately the same number of OSCEs each day (a schedule template is included in Appendix E).
	Notify students of the time and place for the OSCE.
	Print the necessary forms and 3 labels for each student.
	Provide alternatives for any students who need special accommodations.
	Provide training for standardized clients and for the raters.

(continued)

Table 3 (continued)	
Day before	Set up exam site (a set of forms for the examiners, participants, and standardized clients; chairs; pens and pencils).
	If recording, ensure that the video camera is working.
	Ensure that appropriate timing devices (bells, clock for participant and examiners) are working.
Day of OSCE	Arrive early to ensure that rooms are set up properly.
	Provide each student, standardized client, and examiner with the appropriate forms.
	Greet the participants.
	Greet the standardized clients.
	Halfway through the day, debrief with actors and raters so that any changes can be made if necessary.
After the OSCE	Debrief with actors.
	Debrief with instructors.
	Implement the process for monitoring and improving the OSCE.

Budgeting for the OSCE

The cost of running an OSCE for social work has been described as minimal ($40–$70 per student) when the OSCE is integrated into the social work curriculum (Badger & MacNeill, 2002; Miller, 2004). This cost includes training and payment for the standardized client and academic coordinator for one 90-minute interview per student. On the other hand, Hodges et al., (2002), writing about OSCE for medical students, described evaluation as expensive. Through our research and subsequent implementation of the OSCE we have attempted to keep our costs manageable, and therefore the following items do not include the costs of audio or video recording of the OSCE. Our experience has demonstrated that, while involving financial resources, the standardized client program at our medical school has provided significant expertise in constructing scenarios and training the actors so that students experience a fairly standardized client. The budget items to assist in calculating resource needs include recruiting, training, and using standardized clients; appointing contract staff to organize and coordinate all aspects of the OSCE; and buying supplies such as labels, timers, bells, and refreshments for the actors (Sidebar 4).

Depending on the size of the program, number of stations used, and the number of students being tested, the cost of the OSCE can vary significantly. Many teaching universities provide development grants for teaching innovations that can be used to develop scenarios or pilot a simulation project. If only a small number of students will be run through a single-station OSCE, the actor and rater can be trained together and costs kept to a minimum. Additionally, a number of case scenarios are provided for use or adaptation (see Appendix C). Using an established case reduces the cost as well. Because universities are increasingly focused on assessment and outcomes, costs for OSCE can be considered as part of a program's assessment plan (this topic is discussed in Chapter 5). A course fee, similar to a lab fee, might also be charged for each student.

Continuous Refinement of the OSCE and Monitoring Validity and Reliability

The OSCE provides multiple sources of information from which to monitor and improve quality. Student satisfaction measures are known to be influenced by a range of personal variables and therefore are an unreliable source of data to assess the validity of the exam. However, they do provide students' perspectives and, combined with informal feedback from the standardized client, they can be used as another source of data to evaluate and further increase the educational benefits of the OSCE. We modified a student feedback form developed by Miller (2004), which is included in Appendix E. Items measure student satisfaction and ask whether students would have preferred having the OSCE earlier in the social work curriculum and whether they would recommend increasing the number of OSCEs for social work students. Though initially anxious, students have reported high satisfaction with the OSCE experience, being surprised by how real the experience felt, and they indicated that they learned from the experience of actively interviewing (Katz et al., 2014).

Refinement also results from the team of instructors reviewing the OSCE to determine how well the examination assesses the identified competencies; what is the range of student scores and whether the examination differentiates between students who perform at various levels; and what topics, issues, and competencies need more attention in teaching.

Regarding the first point, how well the examination assesses the identified competencies, instructors share impressions based on the experience of using the scales to rate students' performance and reflections. For example, instructors may find that some items are expressed in such a way that all students receive the top rating easily. This may lead to redesigning the items and differentiating more nuanced levels of performance.

Other observations may relate to the ways in which the actors portrayed the standardized clients: Was there enough similarity between the various actors to conclude that the examination was standardized? Was the level of affect and pace of information given appropriate? Did actors respond to students who demonstrated the expected competencies? Were they so forthcoming with information that students did not have the opportunity to demonstrate their skills? These observations will affect training of actors for subsequent OSCEs or point out the need to include additional prompts for the actors so that they display or offer information to which students can respond.

Regarding the reflections, instructors examine how well the questions stimulate narrative material from students which can then be rated on the dimensions on the Reflection Rating Scale. The wording or content of some questions may be changed in an attempt to more specifically elicit and focus the reflection so that the targeted components of the competencies can be assessed.

In addition, statistical procedures can be used to examine the reliability of the scales (see Bogo, Regehr, et al., 2012; Bogo, Regehr, Logie, et al., 2011). Some procedures are establishing internal consistency with Cronbach's alpha and determining interrater reliability and interstation reliability using an intra-class correlation coefficient. These data can provide useful information about scale construction, helping to identify items on the scale that are not reliable and may need refinement. They can also provide information about whether there is consistency between raters and stations.

Establishing the validity of the OSCE can be done in a number of ways. As recommended earlier, content validity can be established by involving expert practitioners in designing and reviewing the content of the client scenarios, including diversity content. Also as noted earlier, it is important to review the consistency or standardization in the actors' presentations. Because different students' styles and responses will elicit somewhat different presentations by the actors, it is important to ensure that all actors use the verbatim statements or prompts. To establish construct validity, in the original project in Toronto, students at various levels of the master's program and experienced social workers participated in a five-station OSCE. As we have described elsewhere,

> Analysis of variance revealed a significant effect of experience for the practice ratings ($F_{2,20} = 4.30$, $p < .05$), with experience level accounting for 30.1% of the variance in participant scores; and a marginally significant effect of experience for the reflection ratings ($F_{2,20} = 3.14$, $p = .06$), with experience level accounting for 23.9% of the variance in participant scores. Post-hoc analysis revealed no differences between current students and recent graduates, but there were significantly higher scores for the experienced practitioners compared with the other two groups on both measures, suggesting some evidence for the construct validity of the OSCE. (Bogo, Regehr, Logie, et al., 2011, p. 12)

Concurrent validity can be examined by comparing the OSCE scores with other measures of competence such as grades in courses or the field practicum (Bogo et al., 2012). Given grade inflation and the recognition that student performance in field is not always actually observed, these comparisons present challenges.

To determine the range of student scores, instructors can calculate and plot the distribution of scores on the Performance Rating Scale and the Reflection

Rating Scale to determine whether the examination can differentiate between students who perform at various levels. In our research we were impressed with the range of scores we found on both scales, unlike the tight clustering of grades and field evaluations (Sowbel, 2011), suggesting that the OSCE can provide a more accurate appraisal of student individual performance. Figures 5 and 6 illustrate this variation from a study comparing OSCE and field evaluation scores (Bogo et al., 2012).

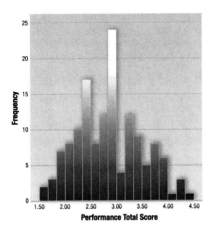
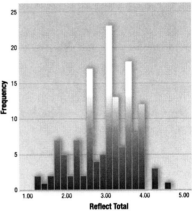

Figure 5. OSCE performance scores. $M = 2.88$; $SD = 0.63$; $N = 140$

Figure 6. OSCE reflection scores. $M = 3.03$; $SD = 0.711$; $N = 138$

Using Findings to Inform Curriculum Development

Finally, based on an analysis of the scores, instructors' observations, and student feedback, instructors will be able to identify topics, issues, and competencies that need more attention in teaching. For example, analyses of student reflections from an OSCE with a simulated client coming out as lesbian indicated varied levels of competence in lesbian, gay, bisexual, and queer affirmative practice (Logie et al., in press). Some students experienced challenges in attitudes (e.g., managing personal reactions), others expressed the need for additional knowledge (e.g., terminology), and many students highlighted the need for skill training (e.g., they did not feel ready to address sexual orientation). These findings shaped recommendations for curriculum development and agency-based training. Other examples from qualitative analyses of students' reflections found that students had difficulty linking explanatory theory to their understanding of the client situations (Katz et al., 2014). Although students could generally label the skills they used and some identified practice principles, they were less likely to be able to conceptualize practice and link that to their actions in the interview. The teaching team decided that they needed to more specifically articulate these links when debriefing classroom role plays or review of video recordings, making stronger connections between practice and theory and illustrating theoretical concepts with related possible practice interventions. In the Azusa Pacific University project, instructors noted the need for greater attention in the classroom to micro interviewing skills. This shift in classroom teaching led to significant improvements in student performance the next year.

In conclusion, developing and implementing a reliable and valid OSCE using standardized clients takes an intentional effort that produces excellent results for assessing competency, enhancing student learning, preparing for and supplementing field education, and supporting curriculum improvement. The opportunity to directly observe students and provide a rating of their performance is rare in social work education in classroom-based courses. Based on our experience and our research, providing students with the opportunity for an authentic experience with an actor trained to play the role of the client in a safe and controlled environment, even if stressful, is an important addition to preparing for practice. The goal of the exam format of the OSCE is to identify areas in which students need further development so that they can be successful in actual practice.

CHAPTER 4

Developing Practice Competence
Through Teaching With Simulation

Simulation in education is the use in teaching of situations that imitate or represent real-life professional practice experiences that students may encounter in the field. As we noted in Chapter 1, simulations involve students in interaction with actors, peers, or instructors who are trained to portray clients in a practice setting in a consistent manner. The interactions can be observed by instructors and other students who provide feedback. When simulations are used in assessment, as in the OSCE, actors portray clients in a standardized manner, and raters use scales to measure dimensions of competence (Bogo et al., 2014). Simulation activities can be used in the classroom to enhance teaching and learning and to prepare students for an OSCE in courses where the OSCE is an assignment. Student engagement with simulation before an OSCE can help develop skills for the examination itself, decrease student anxiety, and result in deeper learning of the material.

When using simulation in courses in the academic setting, this method offers an additional powerful approach to bridge learning in classrooms and in the field. Generally, in classrooms emphasis is placed on conceptual material and critical analysis, whereas in the field students encounter actual experiences of practice with clients and colleagues. In classrooms learning material can be presented and addressed in a structured and systematic manner. In the field learning material is stimulated by the unique circumstances of assigned clients in the particular setting. Field instructors select assignments for students to learn the expected competencies and focus their field instruction not only on these client situations but also in relation to learning objectives required by the university program. However, given the unpredictable and complex nature of clients' needs, learning material cannot be presented in a controlled, systematic manner. Social work educators face the challenge of preparing students with both the needed generic competencies for practice and also the ability to respond flexibly to a wide range of client situations. Thus, simulation experiences that resemble realistic practice events can provide preparation for field learning and also augment it. A unique aspect of simulation is that instructors can design scenarios and remove extraneous issues that may confound learning in real practice situations. Simulations can also be designed to provide data to capture the dimensions of holistic competence discussed in earlier chapters in this text: performance, use of knowledge and social work concepts, and students' internal cognitive and subjective processes.

Additional strengths of learning through the use of simulation are that it provides opportunities for students to practice specific helping processes and skills many times with trained actors, without adverse effects on clients. Educators in health professions have emphasized that learning through simulation is a safe way to prepare practitioners without subjecting patients to potential adverse effects (Trumble, 2012; Ziv, Small, & Wolpe, 2000). Weaver (2011) reviewed studies of simulation in nursing education and found benefits in knowledge, values, and a realistic view of practice.

When simulations are recorded or observed, students, peers, and the instructor can provide feedback and use the simulation to stimulate reflection. Referring to the work of Ericsson, Krampe, and Tesh-Romer (1993; Ericsson, 2004) on deliberate practice, medical educators summarize the benefits of simulation in learning as "effortful repetitive practice of the activity to a mastery level in combination with external constructive feedback" (LeBlanc et al., 2011, p. 4).

Teaching using simulation, especially role play with classmates, has been used extensively in social work education over many decades. As noted earlier in this text, a recent critical review of studies on the use of simulation in social work education found challenges in methodological quality, so recommendations for teaching and assessment are not yet based on a strong empirical foundation (Logie et al., 2013). However, simulation was very well-received by students across all the studies reviewed. Simulation studies included in the review were those that developed standardized client scenarios and used trained actors, drama students, and classmates. Since this review was conducted, we have analyzed our experiences from our more recent studies (Bogo et al., 2012; Bogo, Regehr, Katz, et al., 2011; Bogo, Regehr, Logie, et al., 2011b; Rawlings, 2012) and studies in related fields of medicine and psychology, and we present recommendations for teaching with simulation based on this literature. Our collective experience leads us to highly value the potential of this approach in social work.

Competency-Based Education

In the first two chapters of this text, a competency-based approach to education and assessment is presented that can guide the design of simulation-based teaching and assessment of student learning. Those chapters address the conceptualization and design of a performance-based final assignment to assess and evaluate competence, the OSCE adapted for social work. The OSCE is part of a course design that uses a competency framework and designs educational activities and materials that are well-aligned to the educational outcomes to be assessed. In this way learning goals, objectives, and outcomes, along with educational activities and assessment methods, are integrated and fluid, with each course component reinforcing the others.

Educators are aware that students will study for the test. Studies (Crisp & Green Lister, 2005; Taylor, 1997) find that the method of assessment of student learning significantly influences "what, why, and how students learn and that students will strategically focus on learning that is assessed and seen to 'count'" (Taylor & Bogo, 2013, p. 16). In other words, the method of assessment of student learning will have a powerful influence on what students will do, and hence learn, to prepare for an assignment that has significant weight in a course, such as a final assignment. With this in mind, instructors will do well to pay close attention to the design of final assignments. In this respect, we believe that the OSCE adapted for social work provides one of the best methods for assessing both students' performance and their use of concepts in practice, hence improving the integration of theory and practice. Preparation for the final assignment stimulates and reinforces such learning.

To help students learn the specified competencies and prepare for the final OSCE, we recommend that instructors integrate simulation experiences in the course. If they are doing so, the following specific components of course design and delivery need attention. In teaching, many of these components are integrated. However, for presentation purposes each is discussed separately. These components are (a) course objectives expressed as competencies, (b) creation of a productive socioemotional environment, (c) role induction of students that prepares them to engage in performance-based learning, (d) scenario development, (e) use of various formats for teaching with simulation, (f) debriefing of the simulation with corrective feedback, (g) linkage of theory and practice, and (h) when necessary, supplementation with trained actors in role play, including recommendations for students to prepare and enact client roles with greater authenticity. Even if simulation is used only in the classroom and not used with a formal OSCE, we believe simulation that is observed with debriefing and feedback helps produce deeper learning for students. However, note that having the final OSCE exam motivates students to engage in classroom simulations, knowing they will be evaluated later on those same skills.

Course Objectives Expressed as Competencies

In Chapter 2 there is an extensive discussion of how to design simulations for assessment based on a competency framework. Material in Chapter 2 is useful also for instructors who are interested in using simulation in teaching. To summarize briefly, when educational outcomes are defined as competencies, learning objectives become more transparent. Students become aware of the specific expected learning objectives in a particular course, what these objectives mean in performance or behavioral terms and hence what they will be expected to demonstrate, and how these objectives will be assessed. A body of studies in related health professions education finds that the articulation and specification of competencies enables students to engage more actively and independently in their own learning (McGaghie, Issenberg, Cohen, Barsuj, & Wayne, 2011).

Components of competencies can be expressed at various levels of abstraction: a more general level (e.g., engage with individuals) and at increasingly specific levels that define accompanying practice behaviors (e.g., develop and use a collaborative relationship, use empathy, use interpersonal and interviewing skills). The latter become the further specification of measurable behavioral indicators of students' performance. When course instructors teach competencies, practice behaviors, and related skills (and when they are rating students' mastery on the OSCE), it is useful to keep these various levels in mind. For example, in the Practice Performance Rating Scale in Appendix B, the statement "develops and uses a collaborative relationship" expresses a complex practice at a general level that is then further defined as: clarify the roles of the participants, demonstrate empathic communication, and use diversity in practice. Each of these dimensions is further specified to describe different levels of performance on the rating scale for the final assignment. However, to effectively enact the general competence, these discrete behaviors must be used in an interrelated and holistic manner as the student interacts with the client. A full discussion of the process of articulating competencies and related practice behaviors can be found in Chapter 2.

Creation of a Productive Socioemotional Climate

Creation of a productive socioemotional climate in the classroom is critical to effective use of and engagement with simulation. Pedagogical literature in social work has underscored the importance of a productive socioemotional environment (Anastas, 2010), and therefore it is worthwhile to spend time developing ways of maintaining a positive climate. Classroom environments in social work are generally constructed to include high support and respect. Norms for participation, observation, and constructive ways of giving feedback are developed at the beginning of the course and reviewed regularly. Ideally educational environments with high support provide the foundation for high expectations and high risk. Studies find that students expect their instructors to model these norms and intervene when they are being violated by students in the class (Bogo, Globerman, & Sussman, 2004a).

High risk occurs in the use of simulation because students are expected to conduct interviews while observed by the instructor and peers. In social work, some students express high anxiety related to performance and observation. However, studies in psychology have found that student anxiety related to observation and recording of their interviews with clients in the field is largely a myth. With the caveat that clients must provide informed consent, Ellis (2010) found that most clients are willing to do so if they understand that recordings are confidential and will not be taken out of the setting, and their purpose is to train the student and improve client treatment outcome. Ellis reports that providing role induction regarding supervision expectations reduced anxiety in new supervisees. Role induction involves discussing the processes of supervision and how the approach to teaching relates to learning goals. Importantly, it clarifies what both parties, the student and supervisor, are expected to do. Although Ellis did not find high levels of anxiety even at the beginning of these supervisees' experiences, where higher levels were found they were associated with students who perceived their relationship with their supervisor more negatively. Ellis concludes that relationship factors are probably more important in creating student anxiety than the process of observation.

Based on this literature, both creation of the socioemotional environment and role induction (including students' roles as both a learner and a peer who provides feedback to classmates) are important approaches to prepare for active engagement in performance-based learning. This is especially important for students who prefer a less active and involved learning style, which can be adopted in larger lecture-style classes. A high-support, high-expectation, active, and public learning environment recommended for courses using simulation is one that may engage some students in new ways of learning. Such an environment is also necessary for educational interventions aimed at students' self-understanding and managing emotional self-regulation, an important aspect of practice and of self-care.

The hallmark of competency-based education using simulation is that students have numerous opportunities to practice, debrief, receive feedback and coaching, and incorporate new learning in subsequent practice. A number of teaching methods can be gleaned from the pedagogical literature and from reviews and meta-analysis of studies in psychology on effective methods of teaching helping skills (Hill & Lent, 2006). From educational literature, "instructional guidance rather than pure discovery, and curricular focus rather than unstructured" (Mayer, 2004, p. 14) methods are recommended for promoting learning. From reviews of effective methods for teaching helping skills, Hill and Lent conclude that multiple methods are preferred to a single method, and instruction, modeling, and feedback are effective. Our recommendation to define learning objectives as competencies is similar to Matarazzo's (1978) much earlier review and recommendation to explicitly define behaviors. Also, this review recommended rehearsal and practice, self-observation, and deconditioning of anxiety, similar to the practice of role induction.

In a review in medicine of the effectiveness of teaching with simulation and deliberate practice, there is empirical support for the importance of observation, feedback, and coaching as methods that improve students' performance (McGaghie et al., 2011). Implementation science has identified similar core components for training practitioners to use new evidence-based programs: opportunities to practice new skills, support from peers, modeling, role play, feedback, and coaching (Bearman et al., 2013; Fixsen, Blase, Naoom, & Wallace, 2009). Therefore, instructors need to build in from the outset of the course strong messages about the fact that observation of practice and feedback from peers and instructors are extremely useful ways to learn practice competencies. Later in this chapter, methods for providing feedback are presented.

Role Induction for Students

Because observation by peers and instructors is crucial, to provide authentic feedback students need to learn how to manage their own emotional states, which are often related to performance anxiety. Our studies on social work students' reactions to the OSCE found that most students had high satisfaction with the OSCE, and many spontaneously reported feeling more prepared and more confident about entering the practicum after completing the OSCE assignment (Bogo et al., 2012). However, there was a range in students' ability to regulate their emotional states in the simulated interviews where they were being rated and observed. Although this may not be the case in private interviews, the findings from our analysis of student reflections are instructive in providing suggestions for teaching (Katz et al., 2014). Students at the completion of their first term reflected on their internal states, and descriptions ranged from "extremely nervous" to "calm." Most students noted some initial anxiety at the beginning of the interview but were able to manage these responses by deliberately focusing on the client, listening, and responding and empathizing. Others commented that reminding themselves that they had learned in their course how to interact with and interview a client helped them to see that they could do it. Still other students had difficulty focusing; especially when the client's affect was intense or negative, they found it difficult to relate to the client. Other students reflected that they dealt with their own emotional discomfort about the client's affect by focusing on concrete matters.

In an analysis of the reflections of more advanced students who had completed 1 year or the entire master's program, a continuum of reactions was found (Bogo et al., 2013). The continuum included emotional reactions focused on self in relation to the client, which enabled students to use their own reactions in a purposeful way to understand the client, to pace the interview, and to determine the appropriate focus. At the other end of the continuum were reflections that showed students focused primarily on their own reactions, including their concerns about their lack of experience and confidence to engage with the particular client. This finding is similar to those of other researchers who have studied student anxiety before practicum; they describe student concerns about their lack of knowledge and competence to help clients in the field, and their related fear of humiliation (Gelman, 2004; Gelman, & Lloyd, 2008; Sun, 1999). Furthermore, in our studies some students described feeling so anxious and preoccupied with their own internal state that they had difficulty thinking about the client situation and using the professional knowledge they did have, and they were unable to act in an intentional and potentially useful manner (Bogo et al., 2013). New neuroscience research finds that when one feels emotionally overwhelmed, to the point of experiencing anxiety and insecurity, this emotional state will affect one's ability to cognitively process experiences (Lewis, 2005; Lewis & Todd, 2007).

As many have noted, social work practitioners will confront situations that will provoke strong emotions and play "a significant part in how social workers reason and react" (Munro, 2011, p. 91). Social work educators can help students develop their capacity to understand and increase their ability to tolerate anxiety and insecurity. Simulations and reflections on these scenarios can provide a safe environment in which to explore the emotional reactions to challenging situations and to learn how to tolerate these emotions, be calm and centered, and make use of one's own reactions in practice interventions. Mindfulness has been proposed as one method of achieving emotional self-regulation and can be used in courses where simulation is used. Other methods to help students reduce performance anxiety include deep breathing exercises and visualization. Classroom discussion about the typical feelings of anxiety engendered when they are learning new practices can normalize students' feelings and help them manage feelings of incompetence. Such discussions are educationally focused and avoid crossing boundaries into students' personal lives or becoming quasitherapeutic. Some students will engage more deeply in understanding and attending to their own emotional reactions and may choose to seek individual personal therapy or other helping processes.

Developing Scenarios

Chapter 2 gives a detailed description of the process of designing an OSCE, including scenarios, and readers are advised to review that material. Using the competencies and related practice behaviors as a framework, instructors can work iteratively to design scenarios. Identify the issue, content, and material for each scenario in a way that will provide students the opportunity to practice and learn the necessary behavioral skills.

Preparing actors for the simulation is a crucial part of the method because the power and versatility of the actor are used to achieve the learning goals. In an OSCE the actor aims to provide a standardized portrayal of the client in the scenario, usually in sessions that are approximately 15 minutes long. When teaching with simulation, instructors have the option to have actors participate in a much longer interview; for example, students may take turns, with each interviewing an actor for about 10 minutes in an interview that is continuous. Thus, the actor is less likely to play the role in a standardized manner and must be briefed so that she or he can respond as the interview unfolds, and different students use feedback and coaching that emerges in the previous debriefing to enact the behaviors being taught.

When working with actors it is important to discuss with them what you are trying to achieve in the interviews and to request that they respond positively when the student performs in the way you are trying to teach. For example, if you are teaching the process and skill of exploring feelings, then instruct the actor to respond positively when the student uses appropriate reflections, picks up on cues, and explores implied feeling states. Also useful is to provide the actor with written information such as background and history of the case and emotional state of the client. Regarding the latter, depending on the level of student learning, the actor's emotional expression should be such that students are able to respond. Provide the actor with some verbatim statements that can serve as triggers so that students have the prompts that will enable them to practice the skills the instructor is teaching. For example, if the instructor is aiming to have students use cultural cues in the interview, it is useful to give the actor specific lines about cultural issues pertinent to the scenario.

Using students to enact the scenarios is discussed specifically later in this chapter. Considerations similar to those discussed earlier are important to convey in preparing students to enact the role.

Formats for Using Simulation

Instructors can use a variety of formats when teaching with simulation. Demonstration is considered an important component of learning. Instructors should first interview a simulated client or show a recording of an interview after presenting and discussing concepts, competencies, practice behaviors, and skills. Because opportunities to practice are crucial to learning, students should then have the opportunity to practice interviewing a simulated client. This can occur in class, with students conducting 10 minutes of a long interview, with debriefing taking place after each student interview and also at the completion of the entire interview. It is educationally advantageous if all students have the opportunity to practice interviewing a simulated client. The interviews can be 10 minutes long or longer. When resources allow, such learning activities can be scheduled outside class time and, if video recorded, can be reviewed and discussed in class so that all students can benefit from the instructor's feedback and systematic linkage of practice behaviors to underlying concepts and various components of competence discussed in the course.

Standardized clients in the classroom can also provide the opportunity to observe and practice more specific situations that may not be appropriate for a final exam but are still critical for competency development. For example, engaging a standardized client with suicidal ideation in a classroom setting, either in a generic social work class or in a specialized course in mental health practice, can provide opportunity to learn risk assessment, without harm to an actual client. It also provides students with the opportunity to debrief emotional reactions and self-regulation activities in a higher-risk situation. Role plays with peers, in preparation for work with the simulated client, can help maximize the learning experience, building students' confidence in their abilities and developing their skills as peer evaluators before a simulated client is portrayed by an actor in the classroom. This method is discussed later in the chapter.

Debriefing the Simulation

The provision of feedback has been demonstrated in psychology and implementation science studies to improve learning, especially when accompanied by demonstration, coaching, and guidance about how to do a professional act more effectively (Bearman et al., 2013; Fixsen et al., 2009; Hill & Lent, 2006). Studies on the timing of feedback differ somewhat between fields. Earlier research in social work recommended feedback both during and after an observation of performance (Abbott & Lyter, 1998; Fortune & Abramson, 1993; Freeman, 1985). However, in a study using simulation and feedback to train child welfare workers, Powell, Fisher, and Hughes-Scholes (2008) found greater improvement in the use of open-ended questions when participants received feedback during the interview rather than at the end of the interview. In contrast are findings from studies in medicine involving teaching technical skill. These studies found that summary feedback at the end of a simulation results in better learning outcomes than concurrent feedback (LeBlanc et al., 2011).

Although more research is needed to identify optimal methods for debriefing in social work, the following recommendations may be useful to instructors.

When feedback is provided during an observation, the interview can be stopped, and the instructor or other students can provide suggestions as a form of coaching. When feedback is given after an observed performance, it appears effective when it is more immediate, that is, close in time to the actual performance. Feedback should be based on what was observed and should be balanced, including both positive and critical comments. Comments should be as specific as possible, so it is important to have observers take notes of the session or review an audio or video recording and then provide feedback while all participants view the recording. Objectionable feedback styles are those that are demeaning or harsh or humiliate the student.

Students need to be taught how to give feedback in their role as peer learners. When students are observing their peers, it is helpful to identify specific competencies and practice behaviors to focus on in observations. Beginning students may or may not have enough knowledge and experience to know what to look for or what constitutes good practice. Maintaining a focus on the competency that is being practiced also reinforces the learning objectives for the course. Similar to the discussion in Chapter 3 on training raters, students can also be too harsh or too lenient in their feedback to their peers. A discussion about appropriate feedback can help prevent both tendencies. Feedback can be framed as constructive and not as criticism to help students avoid negatively internalizing feedback but to perceive it as useful for their own development.

Similarly, in studies of group supervision we found that feedback should be structured to avoid ad hoc comments by peers and instructors (Bogo, Globerman, & Sussman, 2004a, 2004b). It should relate to the competencies and practice behaviors being studied. Norms established at the beginning of the course or group should guide students' comments to each other. Students stated that comments from peers that were experienced as patronizing, hurtful, or simply excessive led to reluctance to share examples of practice.

A useful way to conduct the feedback process is to have the student who participated in the simulation begin the debriefing session with his or her own comments, identifying both strengths and instances where the student perceived he or she was not doing well and on reflection would have performed differently. This type of activity may begin to build the capacity for self-assessment. Developing skills in accurate self-appraisal is a critical aspect of effective practice for social work. Continuing professional development for most health and human service professions involves self-assessment despite a growing body of research that finds a large group of individuals are inaccurate in their self-assessment, either underrating or overrating their abilities. For example, in a comprehensive review of research on self-assessment of physicians, 20 rigorous studies were found comparing self and external assessment. Of these, 13 showed little, no, or an inverse relationship; and in a number of studies physicians who were the least skilled were the most confident (Davis et al., 2006). In a study of nursing students' perceptions of their responses in a simulated emergency, the researchers compared students' self-perceptions with ratings on their observed performance (Baxter & Norman, 2011). After a simulation activity, students' confidence and perceived competence increased. However, there was "no evidence of a positive association between self-assessed and observed performance" (p. 2410). The authors recommend caution in relying on self-assessment to determine learning needs and recommend additional strategies, such as OSCEs, to determine areas that should be focused on in clinical learning.

Similarly, in our studies on OSCEs with social work students, recent graduates, and practitioners, we found in some instances a lack of congruence between students' or participants' descriptions and analysis of their performance in their written or verbal reflections when compared with their actual performance. Some students and participants accurately reported on their behavior in the interviews, but others did not. The latter group included students who actually stated that they carried out specific behaviors that the rater stated were not observed or were not found when the researchers reviewed a recording of the interview.

The ability to self-assess appears related to an understanding of the concepts and the ability to use performance behaviors that provide evidence of that understanding. This involves the meta-competence of being able to conceptualize practice and to accurately assess one's level of functioning. Given the findings in the studies on self-assessment reviewed earlier, and given that self-assessment is an important metacompetence, it is worthwhile when using simulation in teaching to spend time in the classroom demonstrating actual performances and helping students develop more accurate ability to assess the expected competencies and skills.

Actors who have been trained in simulation centers usually have also had instruction in how to give feedback to students about their performance. Actors who are not trained in simulation centers can be prepared with guidelines for giving feedback to students. In our experience we have found that this feedback can be useful to the student, especially if it is specific and relates to how the character the actor portrayed may have felt. For example, an actor playing a timid and scared client told the student that when the student went slowly in pacing the interview, asked open-ended questions, and normalized the client's feelings, the client felt understood and supported. This actor was familiar with the competencies the instructor was teaching.

In many instances, when students hear feedback from the actor it has a more powerful effect than when it is provided by an instructor. For example, an actor was able to say to a student that the manner used to engage the client, combined with the height and weight of the student, made the actor feel as if the interviewer were a policeman, and thus this actor was afraid to answer the questions. This served as important feedback to the student and helped him to be aware of how his size affected clients. Based on the actor's comments, the class was able to engage in a productive discussion of self-awareness and use of self. The student was able to practice strategies that emphasized an accentuated, gentle engagement of the client.

Actors whose feedback is based on their own unique personality and preferences should say so, because we found that in some situations actors provide feedback to students that contradict the skills being taught. For example, one actor commented, "I don't like to talk about feelings, I want suggestions," in a class that was aiming to develop students' ability to explore feelings and avoid premature problem solving. As a result, it is important for the instructor to be present when the actor provides feedback, to align the information with course objectives.

If an OSCE is used as a final assignment, summative review of key themes in the interviews, the scenario, and the students' responses can provide significant new learning. To accomplish this, schedule the OSCE a week before the end of the course so that the final class includes debriefing the assignment. The focus should be on the content of the OSCE and student performance and reflections that link to concepts. When debriefing is unstructured in class, we have found that students who struggled on the OSCE have dominated the group discussion by pointing out limitations (e.g., not authentic, difficult actor to engage, own anxiety), despite the confidential student feedback indicating extremely high satisfaction with the OSCE as a learning experience and assessment method (Bogo et al., 2012).

The following process has proven useful. Before the final class, the instructor reviews the OSCE interviews (or feedback on the rating scales and reflections), noting where students demonstrated mastery and where there were mistakes or omissions. In the final class the instructor presents these themes and asks students to state where they struggled in the process of conducting the interview and writing their reflections. Consistent with the findings on self-assessment, students identify some but not all of the themes.

Promoting the Linkage of Theory and Practice

As noted throughout this discussion, simulated situations provide opportunities for students to learn interviewing skills and the way they can be used in enacting complex practice behaviors. Course instructors tend to provide feedback on interviewing skills, and without a doubt this is an important aspect of teaching using simulation. However, using simulation in teaching provides rich information about the client and the student's reaction to the client that can facilitate the student's integration of theory and practice. Returning to the holistic competence model, teaching can explicitly link components of competence, such as underpinning social work theoretical concepts as they emerge (or are designed for simulated clients to portray) in interviews. Recall that holistic competence consists of the integration of numerous crucial elements such as knowledge, values, use of self, ways of thinking, self-reflection, and self-awareness that are evident in what social workers do in practice. Debriefing the simulation in relation to these components can develop students' ability to recognize, examine, and use the social work knowledge and value base, to reflect on how one can manage affective reactions to client material, and to assess one's actual performance of the skills.

As noted earlier in this chapter, analysis was conducted on more than 200 student reflections on their performance in a variety of scenarios in OSCEs. Students in these studies had completed the first term of an MSW program (Bogo et al., 2012; Katz et al., 2014), the first year of the program, or the entire 2 years of the program (Bogo, Regehr, Logie, et al., 2011; Bogo et al., 2013). Differences in students were seen in their ability to conceptualize practice, regulate their emotions, and self-assess their level of performance.

An important finding from these studies was that some students had difficulty conceptualizing practice using explanatory or intervention theory. Reflections of students who completed 1 year or the entire 2 years of the master's program revealed that many were able to use explanatory or intervention theory to discuss the client situation and their practice. Others were comfortable only labeling practice principles and skills. However, some study participants could not use concepts to discuss their practice, chose a range of terms in a haphazard manner, or misused terms (Bogo et al., 2013). For many students who had completed the first term of the first year of the master's program, personal and previous quasiprofessional experiences similar to the client scenario predominated as their method for conceptualizing clients and their situations (Katz et al., 2014). Whereas some use concepts and principles accurately and in some depth, others mention them only in a cursory manner.

The implication of these findings is that it is important for instructors to integrate teaching about skills related to broader notions of competence. Instructors can explicitly draw links between theory and practice and model critical thinking and reflection demonstrating how students can examine their practice through deliberate use of particular concepts. Students can learn to move back and forth from theory to practice. This involves illustrating various concepts with practice examples, which can be demonstrated by developing specific simulations. Also, practice information in simulations can be conceptualized using the lens of various theories. The association between understanding phenomena and the critical thinking involved in choosing appropriate interventions can be articulated. In this way students learn to integrate theory and practice.

In making linkages between theory and practice, it is helpful to consider the level and experience of the student being taught. Younger students and students with less social work experience typically begin with and need more structured and concrete practice behaviors to guide their performance. Theoretical concepts also need to be structured so as to provide a framework for organizing their experiences and perceptions of practice. As students develop their skill and experiences, they are better able to engage in more flexible and reflexive practice that integrates theoretical constructs in practice. With such a foundation, students can benefit enormously from using simulation to learn aspects of specialized and advanced practices.

Use of Role Play With Classmates Playing the Client

Although simulation with trained standardized clients is preferable, given the resource costs, instructors may need to use role plays where a student takes the role of the client. However, students need training to enact roles in an authentic manner, and the following guidelines have been useful.

To prepare for the role play, students are encouraged to choose a situation or scenario with some depth and complexity. The level of difficulty should be realistic considering the stage of development of practice competence of classmates. Instructors can prepare role play scenarios, or students can prepare scenarios based on guidelines from the instructor. In these instances students can write a brief description of the client, including facts and surface information that they can easily provide when asked for by the interviewer, such as, age, gender, socioeconomic information, cultural group identification, relationship status, emotional state, and any other details pertinent to the scenario being played. Such scenarios provide a vehicle for integrating teaching competence for engaging with difference and diversity.

Students are encouraged to do some preliminary thinking and reflect on the client's experience and how the client may feel about the particular issue presented. In this way students may be able to identify with the client and portray the role in an authentic way. Students should prepare a list of a range of complex and nuanced feelings to be conveyed, such as anger and sadness, frustration and inadequacy, wish for connection and fear of intimacy. It can be instructive for the student to enact the same role several times, portraying different emotional states and related behaviors each time, such as passivity, anger, resistance, or open engagement. This method provides the student interviewer with an opportunity to practice a range of interviewing skills, depending on the client's emotional presentation.

When students play client roles, they may divulge all the information or talk in a pressured manner, neither of which provides the opportunity for the student interviewer to practice use of the interviewing and communication skills. Colleagues may help each other out when the skills are not used. Role players are advised to avoid these tendencies, speaking at a moderate pace, not too fast or too slow, inserting short periods of silence, and giving the interviewer some time and space to use the skills to elicit information by asking questions, probing, using follow-up comments, seeking concreteness, and reflecting thoughts and feelings.

The role player should refer to the list of feelings he or she has developed and present some of these feelings fairly directly but also provide subtle suggestions of other feelings so that the interviewer receives the cues and can pick up on and explore implied and underlying feelings. Students are encouraged to respond positively to effective strategies used by the interviewer and adopt a stance that is not overly resistant or difficult. Based on the level of students' development and competencies identified for the course, more complicated scenarios can be designed, including dealing with anger, resistance, and other highly negative states, or more challenging topics such as breaking bad news.

Using Video Recordings of Simulated Practice in Teaching

As the Toronto team was working on developing simulation for assessment, we had the opportunity to meet and interact with Paula David, a social worker and director of the Department of Learning Programs, Haruv Institute, Jerusalem, Israel. This institute provides research and training in the field of child maltreatment to a wide range of practitioners who come in contact with children at risk. David had been experimenting with the use of simulation in training and shared her work, including how she developed scenarios, produced video recordings using simulated interviews, and organized a guest lecture for social work students. This process is clearly described and is included as Appendix F. It can serve as a guide and template for instructors who are interested in using video recordings of simulated practice in teaching. Using such recordings is another way to capitalize on the power of an emotional and realistic simulated encounter to stimulate learning. In David's examples of practice, both effective and ineffective interventions are presented, which can be used for analysis of key concepts and practice principles.

Using Virtual Simulation in Teaching

Simulation using technology is well established in related health professions education where mannequins, devices, and Web-based simulation programs have been successfully designed to train students on a wide range of tasks. Given the expansion of distance education, it is likely that more social work programs will use Web-based technology in teaching (Regan & Youn, 2008). An interesting and thorough description and discussion of the use of Second Life, an online virtual world, to teach engagement and assessment skills for home visits to students in a foundation year direct practice course are provided by Wilson, Brown, Wood, and Farkas (2013). Second Life can simulate practice environments where students use "graphical self-representations (referred to as avatars)" (Wilson et al., 2013, p. 424). This teaching team was supported with technical and administrative resources needed to design an authentic Web-based home visiting scenario, including a script for the client avatar and identification of the skills needed for home visits (including ensuring safety, engaging clients, and conducting an assessment), with an accompanying checklist to guide students' practice in the simulation. Although feedback from students and instructors indicated that it was difficult to use the avatars effectively, they also found the simulation offered useful learning about home visiting. In debriefing participants also recommended more linkage of the concepts taught in the course and the practice experiences in Second Life. This finding is similar to the theme throughout this text regarding the importance of integrating theory and practice when using simulation.

Another promising project using innovative technology is that undertaken by the University of Southern California School of Social Work in its military social work program. A description of the development of its Virtual Patient Avatar for Military Social Work can be found at http://www.youtube.com /watch?v=2OIE7PeAYoc. Through the Center for Innovation and Research on Veterans and Military Families, students who were service members and veterans and clinicians with experience working with veterans are developing believable and realistic dialogues to program into an avatar. The avatar is an electronic virtual image representing a simulated client and is programmed to respond based on the computer user's responses to the virtual scenario presented. Students can practice behaviors related to building a relationship in a safe environment and learn how to demonstrate an understanding of the traumas of returning veterans. Lessons learned in this project will have important implications for using this technology in other specialized areas of social work practice.

To summarize, carefully designed simulation, whether with simulated standardized clients or role plays with peers, provides excellent training opportunities for developing holistic competence. Developing a safe environment for students to engage in authentic simulation allows them to develop competencies that can then be assessed in an OSCE or other final exam, in addition to developing components of competence such as self-regulation, and linkage of theory to practice, necessary for professional social work practice.

CHAPTER 5

Engaging University Partners, Frequently Asked Questions, and Conclusions

Because conducting an OSCE or other simulation exercise takes time and financial resources, engaging university partners and collaborators such as faculty colleagues, deans or directors, and students is critical for success. This chapter provides some suggested strategies that can assist in this process. It is also worth noting that for this initiative, small programs often have the advantage. Although they may have fewer physical and monetary resources, there are often fewer people to involve and convince of the value of the simulation program. Often there is no curriculum committee that must review and approve the addition of such a program, allowing much more flexibility in how the curriculum is designed and implemented and how educational outcomes are assessed.

The following suggestions also apply to using simulation in teaching, but because preparing an OSCE is more detailed and resource intensive, it is likely that more institutional support is needed than for encouraging its use in teaching. Most social work practice instructors are more likely to use role play and simulation with actors, albeit in an informal way.

Social work programs can benefit from the work of scholars who have studied core factors associated with successful implementation of new programs and innovations such as Fixsen et al. (2009). Of relevance to effective adoption of OSCE are staff members who are qualified (or are interested in becoming qualified) to carry out the innovation and are available for training and ongoing consultation, are champions of the project, and provide facilitative administrative support, including developing a receptive organizational culture and climate. Nursing and health policy literature identify the important role of champions as a factor leading to the successful implementation of new approaches by "[convincing] others to accept the innovation" (Soo, Berta, & Baker, 2009, p. 125). Champions in organizations can be in senior leadership positions, responsible for managing departments or units, or front-line clinicians. Some key roles for champions include providing education about the innovation, using empirical evidence to link the innovation to the organization's goals and strategies, and building relationships with those who might use the new approach. We offer the following suggested engagement strategies based on this literature and our own experiences.

Engaging Faculty Colleagues

OSCEs and simulation are most often attached to practice courses for social work students, in both foundation and specialized or advanced courses. Faculty members teaching these courses often have direct practice experience in the field and have an intrinsic desire to participate in the training of competent future social workers. We have found that faculty often desire ways in which to provide direct feedback to students on their developing competencies. Yet as in many institutions, that desire is often constrained by the competing tasks of the academy. When first introduced to faculty, the OSCE can feel like an overwhelming endeavor, and we acknowledge the time commitment, especially for the initial phases. Once the various components have been designed and reviewed, subsequent implementation of the OSCE becomes far less time consuming. It is important to highlight how this process is both doable and efficient; time invested in the OSCE is compensated by less time in other areas, such as grading written exams and papers or watching hours of role play video recordings.

The faculty lead can be seen as the key person to champion the implementation of simulation and OSCE and to work with others to experiment with this innovation. Based on the amount of time spent on this role, release time may be offered. As noted in the literature cited earlier, a champion approach is recommended because such people can consistently present the idea, advocate for its use, and encourage colleagues to try it, offering support and guidance.

As other instructors come on board, a simulation development team can be identified or an informal learning community established.

Identify and Provide Professional Development for a Lead Faculty Member to Champion and Coordinate OSCE Initiatives

Social work programs that identify OSCE as worthy of consideration are likely to have a faculty member who has some interest in and experience with the method. There are many opportunities for further learning, mentoring, and networking so that this person can become more knowledgeable and skilled in the approach. Colleges and universities with health professions education programs are likely to use simulation. With the increased attention to education for interprofessional teams, instructors in a range of health professions may welcome collaborative work with social work. Such colleagues may have already used OSCEs and simulation in their programs, may have expertise that social work faculty can draw on, and may also have labs and related space that they are willing to share with social work programs.

Many local and regional areas throughout North America organize simulation networks, conferences, and courses where faculty members can learn a great deal about using simulation in teaching and assessment. Also, the Society for Simulation in Health Care holds national conferences in North America and abroad. As noted earlier, there is a growing community of social work educators who meet at the CSWE Annual Program Meeting and present their research and offer workshops on simulation and OSCE.

Provide Opportunities for Interested Faculty Members to Explore OSCE Benefits and Gain Expertise in the Method

To interest faculty colleagues in using OSCE, the following points are useful to underscore. The appealing benefits of using simulation in teaching relate to the power of the method and to the growing body of evidence that supports this form of active learning as effective; it is highly motivating for students because it stimulates them to engage in practicing social work and ultimately is likely to develop their overall competence. In courses where OSCE is an assignment, motivation to prepare for the examination is even greater, and students practice frequently, both in classroom activities such as interviewing simulated clients and in role play with peers, knowing they will be assessed on those competencies.

Instructors can teach in a manner that is directly related to students' practice performance (rather than to the reconstruction or analysis of practice in written papers), provide direct feedback, and in students' subsequent and final performances see the effects of their educational interventions. When instructors review student learning outcomes in this way, they gain data that directly inform teaching and curriculum development; topics and behaviors requiring more attention are easily identified and new educational activities designed. This iterative process of curriculum design makes use of educational outcomes in a systematic way.

Pedagogical research in social work is needed to provide an evidence base for our teaching efforts (Bogo, 2012). Simulation in teaching and assessment is a topic needing further understanding and investigation and can provide faculty members interested in the scholarship of teaching and learning with many conceptual and design issues worthy of study. Faculty members in teaching track appointments may want to engage in the scholarship of teaching and learning through a research process. Simulation and OSCE is an interprofessional area worthy of investigation that can reap benefits in producing results that have immediate implications for education. Such research can be facilitated by teams that include teaching faculty and those with research methodological expertise.

As noted earlier in this text, educational outcome assessment receives attention and priority in central administration of colleges and universities. Many institutions will have central teaching support offices, which may be able to provide consultation on developing and studying simulation and OSCEs. Local grant opportunities also may be available to fund program development that would provide seed funds to launch a pilot study.

Engaging Deans and Directors

As noted earlier, those in leadership roles can play a key role in the adoption of innovations (Fixsen et al., 2009; Soo et al., 2009). In social work, in light of the accreditation expectations in EPAS 2008 and 2015 and the worldwide focus on accountability and transparency in higher education, OSCE can provide extremely useful information to address EP 4, "Assessment." Deans and directors are likely to welcome the type of relevant outcome data that can be collected in an OSCE, data that can inform the university and school of the success of the program and inform curriculum decisions and design. As with the introduction and effective use of any new approach, instructors need to have the skills and supports to use innovative educational approaches effectively. Facilitative administrators are needed who will see the value of such an initiative and provide the necessary resources. The support of leadership is critical to empowering the faculty member and champion in charge of the project. Often, although directors may in theory be supportive, they are constrained by their own competing demands for resources. However, resource allocation always involves choices, and often the dean or director has the discretion to invest in an OSCE, even if only on a pilot basis.

It is wise to align social work program activities with institutional priorities. As noted earlier, because interprofessional practice is being emphasized in professional training, social work leadership may want to explore with deans and directors in related health professions education programs how OSCEs can be engaged in from an interprofessional perspective. Also, encouraging faculty members in these programs to do so will be crucial because it is the instructors who will need to work together to design and offer educational and assessment activities.

Elsewhere we have discussed the importance of involving field practicum directors in making the case for the use of simulation in teaching and assessment (Wayne, Bogo, & Raskin, 2015). There are a number of reasons for this recommendation. First, there are fewer field agencies that are able to provide the intensive student supervision of the past with instructors who observe students' practice and provide feedback. Anecdotally, it appears that this traditional model of field instruction may no longer be as universally used as in the past. To ensure the competence of their graduates, programs may require assessment methods in addition to the usual practice of relying on field instructors' evaluations. Second, in light of agency pressures, many settings are reluctant to provide assignments for first-year and beginning students, perceiving that they do not possess the foundation skills. Field directors can point out that students have participated in simulations in practice courses, have successfully completed an OSCE, and are ready to learn to transfer their knowledge and skills into practice with actual clients.

Engaging Students

Students may also need to be engaged in the use of simulation and OSCE in social work. We have found that students can initially show some resistance. Although faculty can use their authority to demand participation in simulation and to require OSCEs, helping students understand the benefits of this method is preferable so that they fully embrace the learning and development opportunities presented. In Chapter 4 we discussed the usefulness of role induction, a process of orienting students to a type of learning where they are actively involved in interviewing simulated clients and providing constructive feedback to peers. Part of this preparation involves conveying messages that students will experience as supportive and that will reduce performance anxiety. Some examples follow.

- Engage in classroom practice opportunities through role plays and simulations with standardized clients.
- Emphasize the benefits of making mistakes with a standardized client before making mistakes with real clients. Because the importance of safety for clients is a concern in social work, simulations will help students learn to interview vulnerable and at-risk people in a low-risk environment.
- Reassure students that faculty and evaluators are aware that they are in the beginning stages of their training.
- Finally, students may benefit from hearing from former students who can share their positive experiences with the OSCE.

Frequently Asked Questions

We began sharing our results and experiences in presentations and faculty development institutes at the CSWE Annual Program Meeting and the

Association of Baccalaureate Social Work Program Directors meeting in 2007. Since that time we have seen an ever-growing community of social work educators who are experimenting with and studying the use of OSCE in assessment and simulation in teaching. In the interests of supporting instructors who are considering implementing an OSCE, this text ends with a series of frequently asked questions from those who have attended our institutes and presentations.

I'm Not at a Large Research University. Can I Still Do This?

Yes! In some ways it can actually be easier to implement with fewer students and faculty members. Remember, offices and classrooms can be used, and we have provided scenarios and rating scales for your use or adaptation. It is still critical to follow the steps in development to align the OSCE with your program's interpretation of competence and practice behaviors, to examine reliability and validity of the test, and to ensure that it is responsive to the local context, mission, and goals of the program.

Do You Teach to the Test?

Yes! The premise of competency-based education is that we are trying to move students toward competence in demonstrating their integration of the knowledge, values, and skills that are presented in the classroom. The more we can prepare students with the various competencies, the better able we will be to determine their skill level. One option is to also provide students with the rating scale before the exam. However, students must be cautioned to avoid interviewing to the scale because it decreases their authentic engagement with the client, thus lowering their score.

Do You Use the Same Scenario Each Year?

You can use the same scenario each year. The selection of a scenario should be guided by the outcomes you want to assess. Instructors have expressed concern that using the same examination each year will bias the results. See further responses to this question later.

What If Students Talk to Each Other About the Exam?

Although we instruct students not to talk to each other about the exam, we are certain that at times they do. However, we have observed that instead of improving performance, it tends to have a negative effect. Rather than being authentically engaged with the client in the scenario, students act in a scripted, practiced fashion that is not responsive to where the client is in the interaction in the interview. We strongly advise students to avoid sharing information about the examination.

Anecdotally, instructors in nursing programs have told us that they have students sign a confidentiality agreement. This agreement is presented to students as an aspect of behaving as a professional, that their professional Code of Ethics underscores the importance of confidentiality and behaving with integrity. Similarly, the National Association of Social Workers Code of Ethics upholds the value of confidentiality, and students could be asked to sign a form indicating they will not share information gathered or observed from their participation in the OSCE. (See the Pledge of Confidentiality in Appendix E.)

What About Negative Student Outcomes?

Some students do poorly in the OSCE and fail the examination. As with all assignments, instructors must decide in advance and communicate in the course outline what weight will be given to performance on the OSCE. Because some students become extremely anxious when being observed and perform poorly, instructors will want to consider whether the OSCE is one of a number of assignments used in calculating the final grade. Though affected by stress, poor performance may still indicate a lack of competence. If the program accepts responsibility for determining that students are ready to enter the field practicum, proceed to the next level in the program, or graduate, then remediation followed by another opportunity to repeat the OSCE is necessary.

We have had experiences where the student's anxiety about being directly observed has negatively affected performance. In these situations, we have not rated the student well. It is important to debrief with the student and explore what the experience was like for him or her and consider whether there is an opportunity to assist the student with self-regulation. It has also been helpful to gain more information from the course instructor or others who have had experience with that student who can provide insight into whether the performance reflected the student's general skill level. When poor skill was also evident in the classroom, we have offered remedial intervention to prepare the student for field education, or in some cases the student chose not to continue in social work. We have also had instances of poor performance that were not felt to be indicative of student skill, and the student was advanced to field education.

It is important to consider whether the program will share information on student performance with the field instructor. Practicum directors have often found that university privacy policies require them to withhold significant information. If field instructors subsequently learn that they have not been privy to information that might have facilitated their ability to help students learn, they understandably have registered concern with the program. The Toronto team believed that it was extremely useful and desirable to include field instructors as part of the educational team. They worked with university lawyers to develop appropriate written communications to students in clear language that did not disregard relevant privacy legislation. Students were informed that written evaluations of their performance in a practice course, including the OSCE, would be shared with the field instructor. The intention is to bridge learning with simulation and learning in the field practicum. Areas of strength and areas needing more development are identified so that students and field instructors can incorporate this information as learning goals in the field contract. The faculty field liaison reviews both these documents to ensure the inclusion of past learning issues and goals and provide necessary supports. This approach is discussed in Chapter 3, and Appendix D includes the Social Work Practice Laboratory Course SWK 4105 Final Feedback Form.

Both of our teams have examined the relationship between outcomes on the OSCE and on field performance and found that all students who had difficulty in the field also had difficulty on the OSCE (Bogo et al., 2012; Rawlings & Johnson, 2012). However, not all students who did poorly on the OSCE did poorly in the field. We speculate on the meaning of the specific findings reported in Bogo et al. (2012) in Chapter 1.

Can I Assess Student Performance Through a One-Way Mirror?

Instructors have often asked this question, wanting to be sensitive to students' feelings of anxiety and fear of evaluation. We in social work education need to challenge the assumption that students cannot handle the anxiety associated with being observed. Indeed, elsewhere (Wayne, Bogo, & Raskin, 2010) we have commented on Lee Shulman's (2005) seminal work on signature pedagogy where he points out that anxiety can be adaptive and viewed as a necessary feature of learning. "Uncertainty, visibility, and accountability inevitably raise the emotional stakes of the pedagogical encounters" (Shulman, 2005, p. 57), and students are likely to experience some anxiety, which can serve as a motivator for harder work in preparing for practice, simulated interviews, and the OSCE. Students will also feel anxiety when they first start meeting with clients in their field practicum. Yet for students to grow and improve over the course of their career, they need to become comfortable with evaluation and feedback. A well-planned simulation, with accurate and supportive feedback, can go a long way in socializing students to be transparent in their learning both in the classroom and with future supervisors. We need to socialize our students, similar to those in related health professions such as medicine and nursing, to having their performance directly evaluated.

Furthermore, we have found that being in the room with the student and standardized client provides a more accurate picture of the felt experience than sitting behind a mirror and much more so than can be captured on a video recording.

Can I Use Other Students From the University to Play the Role of the Standardized Client?

We have found that people trained in acting are preferred and engage the role in a much more authentic way. The principle is that we want the standardized client to feel like a real client in every way. Students have commented on how real the scenario seemed and how superior this experience was to that of role playing with peers. Trained actors have at times shed tears and developed impromptu responses that amazed us.

We strongly advise against using other students, particularly if you are at a small university. You do not want students to have an exam with someone they might know from another context. This is unfair for the student. That said, if you are at a very large university, then it may be possible to arrange an exchange with the drama department. At simulation conference presentations we have heard of collaboration between psychology and drama departments where drama students' assignments involved acting as a simulated client for psychology students' assignments. Faculty in both departments would need to develop relevant educational goals and methods of training drama students to enact particular types of scenarios and clients.

Conclusion

The adoption of a competence framework for accrediting schools of social work by the CSWE in the United States in 2008 also included attention to assessment of educational outcomes. This change stimulated the social work education community to search for more effective methods to determine whether our programs and educational efforts were effective in developing the next generation of social workers. The authors of this text became interested in moving beyond traditional assessment methods such as field evaluations, written papers, and examinations and began to explore the potential use of simulation.

Simulation has been used effectively in related health and human service professions to assess performance and appeared to offer promise for social work educators. Using simulation in teaching is not new, as social work educators have used variations of this method, including role play, for decades. However, using simulation in the assessment of student learning is largely a new innovation and requires those of us in social work education to further develop effective methods. It requires a systematic approach based on clear conceptualization of competence and desired outcomes, articulated in measurable terms, and the creation of a range of reliable, valid, and authentic materials so that one can have confidence in the method and results it yields. Used effectively in health professions, the OSCE offers social work educators one such method for assessment of student competence in key areas of direct practice. The addition of a reflective process, either as a dialogue or in written form, provides a means for also assessing other components of competence such as the nature of students' cognitive and subjective processes, critical thinking and emotional and subjective reactions, all of which contribute to the way in which one exercises professional judgment and makes crucial decisions in practice. These are key components of a holistic model of competence, necessary for effective social work practice, and are part of social work programs' stated learning outcomes for students. Higher education institutions recognize that we are in an era of greater expectations and demands to demonstrate accountability. Professional programs have the additional responsibility of graduating professionals who can work effectively and ethically with individuals, families, groups, organizations, and communities. Social work education must continue to develop innovative and effective strategies for assessing student competence.

This book has sought to provide social work educators with the conceptual and practical tools necessary to develop methods and programs of simulation using standardized clients for use in both assessment and teaching of students. As the teams involved benefited greatly from their locations in a large research university and a midsized teaching university, both perspectives were intentionally presented throughout the text to demonstrate how this method is accessible for all who have the interest and passion to champion this innovation at their respective schools.

The initial development of reliable and valid simulation programs can require both time and monetary resources. Accordingly, and because we are committed to champion this method in social work education, we have provided as many resources as we can to the readers of this text. The appendices include planning materials and forms, developed cases, and assessment measures that we have used in our own work. We hope colleagues will use and adapt these materials and also share the materials they create. This development work will provide the foundation for empirical studies to examine the pedagogy of using simulation in teaching and in assessment in social work.

Undertaking an OSCE and teaching with simulation has proven to be highly effective for the two teams whose work is the basis of this text and for faculty colleagues involved in further efforts in using simulation. Based on our own experiences in assessing student competence, as well as the research from both of our teams and from the literature in related health professions, we believe that the OSCE has moved assessment in social work forward. It can provide better information to guide student learning and to focus and improve our teaching and curriculum development. We expect that, as in related health professions' education, the future will see an ever-growing community of social work educators and researchers who will continue to build an evidence base and innovative ways of using simulation in social work.

REFERENCES

Abbott, A. A., & Lyter, S. C. (1998). The use of constructive criticism in field supervision. *The Clinical Supervisor, 17*(2), 43–57.

ACOSA. (2013) *Advanced practice in macro social work.* Retrieved from http://www .cswe.org/File.aspx?id=70501

Aeder, L., Altshuler, L., Kachur, E., Barrett, S., Hilfer, A., Koepfer, S.,... Shelov, S. P. (2007). The "Culture OSCE": Introducing a formative assessment into a postgraduate program. *Education for Health, 20*(1), 1–11.

Alperin, D. E. (1996). Empirical research on student assessment in field education: What have we learned? *The Clinical Supervisor, 14*(1), 149–161. doi:10.1300/ J001v14n01_11

Anastas, J. (2010). *Teaching in social work: An educators' guide to theory and practice.* New York, NY: Columbia University Press.

Arkava, M. L., & Brennan, E. C. (Eds.). (1976). *Competency-based education for social work: Evaluation and curriculum issues.* New York, NY: Council on Social Work Education.

Association of Community Organization and Social Administration. (n.d.). *Advanced practice in macro social work.* Retrieved from www.cswe.org/File .aspx?id=70501

Austin, Z., O'Byrne, C., Pugsley, J., & Quero Munoz, L. (2003). Development and validation processes for an objective structured clinical examination (OSCE) for entry-to-practice certification in pharmacy: The Canadian experience. *American Journal of Pharmaceutical Education, 67*(3), Article 76. doi:10.5688/aj670376

Badger, L. W., & MacNeil, G. (2002). Standardized clients in the classroom: A novel instructional technique for social work educators. *Research on Social Work Practice, 12,* 364–374. doi: 10.1177/1049731502012003002

Baer, B. L., & Frederico, R. (1978). *Educating the baccalaureate social worker.* Cambridge, MA: Ballinger.

Banta, T. (2013). *Assessment: Putting principles into practice.* Paper presented at Council on Social Work Education, Annual Program Meeting, Dallas, TX.

Barrows, H. S. (2000a). *Problem-based learning applied to medical education.* Springfield, IL: Southern Illinois University School of Medicine.

Barrows, H. S. (2000b). *Stimulated recall: Personalized assessment of clinical reasoning.* Springfield, IL: Southern Illinois University School of Medicine.

Baxter, P., & Norman, G. (2011). Self-assessment or self-deception? A lack of association between nursing students' self-assessment and performance. *Journal of Advanced Nursing, 67*(11), 2406–2413. doi:10.1111/j.1365-2648 .2011.05658.x

Bearman, A. K., Weisz, J. R., Chorpita, B. F., Hoagwood, K., Ward, A., & Ugueto, A. M. (2013). More practice, less preach? The role of supervision processes and therapist characteristics in EBP implementation. *Administrative Policy in Mental Health.* doi:10.1007/s10488-013-0485-5

Bennett, L., & Coe, S. (1998). Social work field instructor satisfaction with faculty field liaison. *Journal of Social Work Education, 34*(3), 345–353.

Bogo, M. (2006). *Social work practice: Concepts, processes, and interviewing.* New York, NY: Columbia University Press.

Bogo, M. (2010). *Achieving competence in social work through field education.* Toronto, ON: University of Toronto Press.

Bogo, M. (2012). Editorial: Cultivating scholarship and research in social work pedagogy. *Social Work Education, 31*(4), 403–405. doi:10.1080/02615479 .2012.678767

Bogo, M. (2015). Evaluation of student learning. In C. A. Hunter, J. K. Moen, & M. S. Raskin (Eds.), *Foundations for excellence: Social work field directors* (pp. 154–178). Chicago, IL: Lyceum Books.

Bogo, M., Globerman, J., & Sussman, T. (2004a). The field instructor as group worker: Managing trust and competition in group supervision. *Journal of Social Work Education, 40,* 13–26. doi:10.1080/10437797.2004.10778476

Bogo, M., Globerman, J., & Sussman, T. (2004b). Field instructor competence in group supervision: Students' views. *Journal of Teaching in Social Work, 24*(1/2), 199–216. doi:10.1300/J067v24n01_12

Bogo, M., & Katz, E. (2012). *Reflection questions following interview.* Toronto, ON, Canada: Factor-Inwentash Faculty of Social Work.

Bogo, M., Katz, E., Logie, C., Regehr, C., & Regehr, G. (2012). *OSCE for social work practice performance rating scale.* Toronto, ON, Canada: Factor-Inwentash Faculty of Social Work.

Bogo, M., Katz, E., Regehr, C., Logie, C., Mylopoulos, M., & Tufford, L. (2013). Toward understanding meta-competence: An analysis of students' reflections on their simulated interviews. *Social Work Education, 32*(2), 259–273. doi:10.1080/02615479.2012.738662.

Bogo, M., Logie, C., & Katz, E. (2009). Conceptual mapping of competencies in social work OSCEs: A guide for developing and conceptualizing case scenarios. Toronto, ON, Canada: Factor-Inwentash Faculty of Social Work.

Bogo, M., Mylopoulos, M., Katz, E., Logie, C., Regehr, C., & Regehr, G. (2009). *Reflection questions following interview.* Toronto, ON, Canada: Factor-Inwentash Faculty of Social Work.

Bogo, M., Regehr, C., Hughes, J., Power, R., & Globerman, J. (2002). Evaluating a measure of student field performance in direct service: Testing reliability and validity of explicit criteria. *Journal of Social Work Education, 38,* 385–401.

Bogo, M., Regehr, C., Katz, E., Logie, C., Mylopoulos, M., & Regehr, G. (2011). Developing a tool to assess student reflections. *Social Work Education, 30*(2), 186–195. doi:10.1080/02615479.2011.540392

Bogo, M., Regehr, C., Katz, E., Logie, C., Tufford, L., & Litvack, A. (2012). Evaluating the use of an objective structured clinical examination (OSCE) adapted for social work. *Research on Social Work Practice, 22*(4), 428–436. doi:10.1177/1049731512437557

Bogo, M., Regehr, C., Logie, C., Katz, E., Mylopoulos, M., & Regehr, G. (2011). Adapting objective structured clinical examinations to assess social work students' performance and reflections. *Journal of Social Work Education, 47,* 5–18. doi:10.5175/JSWE.2011.200900036

Bogo, M., Regehr, C., Power, R., Hughes, J., Woodford, M., & Regehr, G. (2004). Toward new approaches for evaluating student field performance: Tapping the implicit criteria used by experienced field instructors. *Journal of Social Work Education, 40,* 417–426. doi:10.1080/10437797.2004.10672297

Bogo, M., Regehr, C., Power, R., & Regehr, G. (2007). When values collide: Providing feedback and evaluating competence in social work. *The Clinical Supervisor, 26*(1/2), 99–117. doi:10.1300/J001v26n01_08

Bogo, M., Regehr, C., Woodford, M., Hughes, J., Power, R., & Regehr, G. (2006). Beyond competencies: Field instructors' descriptions of student performance. *Journal of Social Work Education, 42,* 579–593. doi:10.5175 /JSWE.2006.200404145

Bogo, M., Shlonsky, A., Lee, B., & Serbinski, S. (2014). Acting like it matters: A scoping review of simulation in child welfare training. *Journal of Public Child Welfare, 8*(1), 1–24. doi:10.1080/15548732.2013.818610

Bogo, M., & Vayda, E. (1998). *The practice of field instruction in social work: Theory and process.* Toronto, ON: University of Toronto Press and Columbia University Press.

Boitel, C. (2002). *Development of a scale to measure learning in field education.* Doctor of Philosophy, Case Western Reserve University, Cleveland, OH.

Boud, D., & Knights, S. (1996). Course design for reflective practice. In N. Gould & I. Taylor (Eds.), *Reflective learning for social work* (pp. 23–34). Aldershot, England: Arena.

Cant, R., McKenna, L., & Cooper, S. (2013). Assessing preregistration nursing students' clinical competence: A systematic review of objective measures. *International Journal of Nursing Practice, 19*(2), 163–176. doi:10.1111/ijn.12053

Carraccio, C., Wolfsthal, S. D., Englander, R., Ferentz, K., & Martin, C. (2002). Shifting paradigms: From Flexner to competencies. *Academic Medicine, 77*(5), 361–367.

CASWE-ACFTS. (2013). *Standards for accreditation.* Ottawa, ON: Canadian Association for Social Work Education. Retrieved from http://caswe-acfts.ca/ wp-content/uploads/2013/03/CASWE.ACFTS_.Standards.Oct2013.pdf

Centre for the Evaluation of Health Professionals Educated Abroad. (2011) *Leveling the Playing Field for International Medical Graduates.* Retrieved from http://www.cehpea.ca/examinations/index.htm

Cheetham, G., & Chivers, G. (1996). Towards a holistic model of professional competence. *Journal of European Industrial Training, 20*(5), 20–30. doi:10.1108/03090599610119692

Cheetham, G., & Chivers, G. (1998). The reflective (and competent) practitioner: A model of professional competence which seeks to harmonise the reflective practitioner and competence-based approaches. *Journal of European Industrial Training, 22*(7), 267–276. doi:10.1108/03090599810230678

Cheetham, G., & Chivers, G. (2005). *Professions, competence and informal learning.* Cheltenham, UK: Edward Elgar.

Clark, F., & Arkava, M. (1979). *The pursuit of competence in social work*. San Francisco, CA: Jossey-Bass.

Clark, S. (2003). The California collaboration: A competency-based child welfare curriculum project for master's social workers. *Journal of Human Behavior in the Social Environment, 7*(1), 135–157.

College of Social Work (TCSW). (2012a). Domains within the PCF_Version1 01/05/2012. Retrieved from http://www.tcsw.org.uk/understanding-the-pcf/

College of Social Work (TCSW). (2012b). An introduction to qualifying standards and professional social work education. Retrieved from www.collegeofsocialwork.org/professional-development/educators/

College of Social Work (TCSW). (2014). Retrieved from http://www.tcsw.org.uk/about-us/mission-statement/

Council on Social Work Education. (2008). *Advanced gero social work practice*. Retrieved from http://www.cswe.org/CentersInitiatives/GeroEdCenter/TeachingTools/Competencies/PracticeGuide.aspx

Council on Social Work Education. (2009). *Advanced social work practice in clinical social work*. Retrieved from http://www.cswe.org/File.aspx?id=26685

Council on Social Work Education. (2010). *Advanced social work practice in military social work*. Retrieved from http://www.cswe.org/File.aspx?id=42466

Council on Social Work Education. (2012). *Advanced social work practice in trauma*. Retrieved from http://www.cswe.org/File.aspx?id=63842

Council on Social Work Education. (2008). *Educational policy and accreditation standards*. Retrieved from http://www.cswe.org/Accreditation/2008EPASDescription.aspx

Council on Social Work Education. (2013). *A guide to reviewing draft 1 2015 education policy and accreditation standards (EPAS)*. Retrieved from http://www.cswe.org/File.aspx?id=69945

Council on Social Work Education. (2014). *Draft 2 of the 2015 educational policy and accreditation standards*. Retrieved from www.cswe.org/File.aspx?id=72120

Crisp, B. R., & Green Lister, P. (2005). Walking the assessment tightrope. In H. C. Burgess & I. J. Taylor (Eds.), *Effective learning and teaching in social policy and social work* (pp. 82–94). Abingdon, Oxford, England: Routledge Falmer.

Crisp, B. R., & Lister, P. G. (2002). Assessment methods in social work education: A review of the literature. *Social Work Education, 21*(2), 259–269. doi:10.1080/02615470220126471

Damron Rodriguez, J. (2008). Developing competence for nurses and social workers. *American Journal of Nurses, 108*(9), 27–37. doi:10.1097/01. NAJ.0000336413.83366.e0

Davis, D. A., Mazmanian, P. E., Fordis, M., Harrison, R. V., Thorpe, K. E., & Perrier, L. (2006). Accuracy of physician self-assessment compared with observed measures of competence: A systematic review. *Journal of the American Medical Association, 296,* 1094–1102. doi:10.1001/jama.296.9.1094

de Boer, C., & Coady, N. (2007). Good helping relationships in child welfare: Learning from stories of success. *Child and Family Social Work, 12,* 32–42. doi:10.1111/j.1365-2206.2006.00438.x

Dewey, J. (1933). *How we think.* Boston, MA: D.C. Heath.

Ellis, M. V. (2010). Bridging the science and practice of clinical supervision: Some discoveries, some misconceptions. *The Clinical Supervisor, 29*(1), 95–116. doi:10.1080/07325221003741910

Epstein, R. M., & Hundert, E. M. (2002). Defining and assessing professional competence. *Journal of the American Medical Association, 287*(2), 226–235. doi:10.1001/jama.287.2.226

Eraut, M. (1994). *Developing professional knowledge and competence.* London, UK: Falmer Press.

Eraut, M. (2002). Editorial. *Learning in Health and Social Care, 1*(1), 1–5.

Eraut, M. (2004). Editorial: The practice of reflection. *Learning in Health and Social Care, 3*(2), 47–52.

Ericsson, K. A. (2004, October). Deliberate practice and the acquisition and maintenance of expert performance in medicine and related domains. *Academic Medicine, 79*(10 suppl), 570–581.

Ericsson, K. A., Krampe, R. T., & Tesh-Romer, C. (1993). The role of deliberate practice in the acquisition of expert performance. *Psychological Review, 100,* 363–406. doi:10.1037/0033-295X.100.3.363

Eva, K. W., & Regehr, G. (2005). Self-assessment in the health professions: A reformulation and research agenda. *Academic Medicine, 80*(10 suppl), S46–S54.

Fernandez, N., Dory, V., Ste-Marie, L. G., Chaput, M., Charlin, B., & Boucher, A. (2012). Varying conceptions of competence: An analysis of how health sciences educators define competence. *Medical Education, 46,* 357–365. doi:10.1111/j.1365-2923.2011.04183.x

Finch, J., & Taylor, I. (2013). Failure to fail? Practice educators' emotional experiences of assessing failing social work students. *Social Work Education, 32*(2), 244–258. doi:10.1080/02615479.2012.720250

Fixsen, D. L., Blase, K. A., Naoom, S. F., & Wallace, F. (2009). Core implementation components. *Research on Social Work Practice, 19*(5), 531–540. doi:10.1177/1049731509335549

Fleming, D. (1991). The concept of meta-competence. *Competence and Assessment, 16,* 9–12.

Forgey, M. A., Badger, L., Gilbert, T., & Hansen, J. (2013). Using standarized clients to train social workers in intimate partner violence assessment. *Journal of Social Work Education, 49,* 292–306. doi:10.1080/10437797.2013.768482

Fortune, A. E., & Abramson, J. S. (1993). Predictors of satisfaction with field practicum among social work students. *The Clinical Supervisor, 11*(1), 95–110.

Fouad, N. A., Grus, C. L., Hatcher, R. L., Kaslow, N. J., Hutchings, P. S., Madson, M. B., . . . Crossman, R. E. (2009). Competency benchmarks: A model for understanding and measuring competence in professional psychology across training levels. *Training and Education in Professional Psychology, 3*(4 Suppl), S5–S26. doi:10.1037/a0015832

Fox, R. (2011). *The use of self: The essence of professional education.* Chicago, IL: Lyceum.

Frank, J. R., Mungroo, R., Ahmad, Y., Wang, M., Rossi, S., & Horsley, T. (2010). Toward a definition of competency-based education in medicine: A systematic review of published definitions. *Medical Teacher, 32*(8), 631–637. doi:10.3109/0142159X.2010.500898

Frank, J. R., Snell, L. S., Cate, O. T., Homboe, E., Carraccio, C., & Swing, S. R. (2010). Competency-based medical education: Theory to practice. *Medical Teacher, 32*(8), 638–645. doi:10.3109/0142159X.2010.501190

Freeman, E. (1985). The importance of feedback in clinical supervision: Implications for direct practice. *The Clinical Supervisor, 3*(1), 5–26.

Gaba, D. M. (2007). The future vision of simulation in healthcare. *Simulation in Healthcare, 2,* 126–135. doi:10.1097/01.SIH.0000258411.38212.32

Gelman, C. R. (2004). Anxiety experienced by foundation-year MSW students entering field placement: Implications for admissions, curriculum, and field education. *Journal of Social Work Education, 40*(1), 39–54. doi:10.1080/10437797.2004.10778478

Gelman, C. R., & Lloyd, C. M. (2008). Field notes—Pre-placement anxiety among foundation-year MSW students: A follow-up study. *Journal of Social Work Education, 44*(1), 173–183. doi:10.5175/JSWE.2008.200600102

Gingerich, W. J., Kaye, K. M., & Bailey, D. (1999). Assessing quality in social work education: Focus on diversity. *Assessment and Evaluation in Higher Education, 24*(2), 119–129. doi:10.1080/0260293990240202

Govaerts, M. J., van der Vleuten, C. P., & Schuwirth, L. W. (2002). Optimising the reproducibility of a performance-based assessment test in midwifery education. *Advances in Health Sciences Education, 7*(2), 133–145. doi:10.1023/A:1015720302925

Graham, R., Bitzer, L. A. Z., & Anderson, O. R. (2013). Reliability and predictive validity of a comprehensive preclinical OSCE in dental education. *Journal of Dental Education, 77*(2), 161–167.

Gross, G. M. (1981). Instructional design: Bridge to competence. *Journal of Education for Social Work, 17*(3), 66–74. doi:10.1080/00220612.1981 .10672054

Gursansky, D., & Le Sueur, E. (2011). Conceptualizing field education in the twenty-first century: Contradictions, challenges and opportunities. *Social Work Education, 31*(7), 914–931. doi:10.1080/02615479.2011.595784

Hackett, S. (2001). Educating for competency and reflective practice: Fostering a conjoint approach in education and training. *Journal of Workplace Learning, 13*(3), 103–112. doi:10.1108/13665620110388406

Hall, D. T. (1986). *Career development in organisations*. San Francisco, CA: Jossey-Bass.

Hamilton, J. (2009). Intercultural competence in medical education: Essential to acquire, difficult to assess. *Medical Teacher, 31*(9), 862–865.

Harden, R. M., Crosby, J. R., Davis, M. H., & Friedman, M. (1999). AMEE Guide No. 14: Outcome-based education: Part 5. From competency to meta-competency: A model for specification of learning outcomes. *Medical Teacher, 21*(6), 546–552. doi:10.1080/01421599978951

Harden, R. M., & Gleeson, F. A. (1979). Assessment of clinical competence using an observed structured clinical examination. *Medical Education, 13*, 41–47. doi:10.1136/pmj.2003.011718

Hatcher, R. L., & Lassiter, K. D. (2007). Initial training in professional psychology: The practicum competencies outline. *Training and Education in Professional Psychology, 1*(1), 49–63. doi:10.1037/1931-3918.1.1.49

Hill, C. E., & Lent, R. W. (2006). A narrative and meta-analytic review of helping skills training: Time to revive a dormant area of inquiry. *Psychotherapy: Theory, Research, Practice, Training, 43*(2), 154–172. doi:10.1037/0033-3204.43.2.154

Hodges, B., Hanson, M., McNaughton, N., & Regehr, G. (2002). Creating, monitoring, and improving a psychiatry OSCE. *Academic Psychiatry, 26*(3), 134–161. doi:10.1176/appi.ap.26.3.134

Hodges, B., Hollenberg, E., McNaughton, N., Hanson, M. D., & Regehr, G. (2014). The psychiatry OSCE: A 20-year retrospective. *Academic Psychiatry, 38,* 26–34. doi:10.1007/s50596-013-0012-8

Hodges, B. D. (2006). The objective structured clinical examination: Three decades of development. *Journal of Veterinary Medical Education, 33*(4), 571–577. doi:10.3138/jvme.33.4.571

Hodges, B. D., & Lingard, L. (Eds.). (2012). *The question of competence.* Ithaca, NY: Cornell University Press.

Holloway, S., Black, P., Hoffman, K., & Pierce, D. (2009). Some considerations of the import of the 2008 EPAS for curriculum design. Retrieved from http://www.cswe.org/File.aspx?id=31578

Immordino-Yang, M. H., & Damasio, A. (2007). We feel, therefore we learn: The relevance of affective and social neuroscience to education. *Mind, Brain and Education, 1*(1), 3–10. doi:10.1111/j.1751-228X.2007.00004.x

Jones, A., Pegram, A., & Fordham-Clarke, C. (2010). Developing and examining an objective structured clinical examination. *Nurse Education Today, 30,* 137–141. doi:10.1016/j.nedt.2009.06.014

Kahneman, D. (2011). *Thinking, fast and slow.* New York, NY: Farrar, Straus and Giroux.

Kane, M. T. (1992). The assessment of professional competence. *Evaluation in the Health Professions, 15*(2), 163–182. doi:10.1177/016327879201500203

Kaslow, N. J., Borden, K. A., Collins, F. L. Jr., Forrest, L., Illfelder-Kaye, J., Nelson, P. D., . . . Willmuth, M. E. (2004). Competencies conference: Future directions in education and credentialing in professional psychology. *Journal of Clinical Psychology, 60*(7), 699–712. doi:10.1002/jclp.20016

Katz, E., Tufford, L., Bogo, M., & Regehr, C. (2014). Illuminating students' pre-practicum conceptual and emotional states: Implications for field education. *Journal of Teaching in Social Work, 34,* 96–108.

Kelly, J., & Horder, W. (2001). The how and why: Competences and holistic practice. *Social Work Education, 20*(6), 689–699. doi:10.1080/02615470120089861

Kilpatrick, A. C., Turner, J., & Holland, T. P. (1994). Quality control in field education: Monitoring students' performance. *Journal of Teaching in Social Work, 9*(1/2), 107–120. doi:10.1300/J067v09n01_08

Kolb, D. A. (1984). *Experiential learning: Experience as the source of learning and development*. Englewood Cliffs, NJ: Prentice Hall.

Kwong, M. H. (2012). Incorporating multicultural learning in clinically-based education in the United States. *Social Work Education, 31*(7), 848-865. doi: http://dx.doi.org/10.1080/02615479.2011.599840

Larrison, T. E., & Korr, W. S. (2013). Does social work have a signature pedagogy? *Journal of Social Work Education, 49*(2), 194–206. doi:10.1080/10437797.2013.768102

LeBlanc, V. R., Bould, M. D., McNaughton, N., Brydges, R., Piquette, D., & Sharma, B. (2011). *Simulation in postgraduate medical education*. Retrieved from http://www.afmc.ca/pdf/fmec/18_LeBlanc_Simulation%20and%20Technology.pdf

Lee, C. D., & Ayon, C. (2004). Is the client–worker relationship associated with better outcomes in mandated child abuse cases? *Research on Social Work Practice, 14*(5), 351–357. doi:10.1177/1049731504265833

Lewis, M. (2005). Bridging emotion theory and neurobiology through dynamic systems modeling. *Behavioral and Brain Sciences, 28,* 169-245.

Lewis, M. & Todd, R. (2007). The self-regulating brain: Cortical-subcortical feedback and the development of intelligent action. *Cognitive Development, 22,* 406-430.

Lister, P. G., Dutton, K., & Crisp, B. R. (2005). Assessment practices in Scottish social work education: A practice audit of Scottish universities providing qualifying social work courses. *Social Work Education, 24*(6), 693–711. doi:10.1080/02615470500185135

Logie, C., Bogo, M., & Katz, E. (in press). "I didn't feel equipped": Social workers' reflections on a simulated client "coming out." *Journal of Social Work Education.*

Logie, C., Bogo, M., Regehr, C., & Regehr, G. (2013). A critical appraisal of the use of standardized client simulations in social work education. *Journal of Social Work Education, 49*(1), 66–80. doi:10.1080/10437797.2013.755377

Lu, Y. E., Ain, E., Chamorro, C., Chang, C., Feng, J. Y., Fong, R., . . . Yue, M. (2011). A new methodology for assessing social work practice: The adaptation of the objective structured clinical evaluation (SW-OSCE). *Social Work Education, 30*(2), 170–185. doi:10.1080/02615479.2011.540385

Maidment, J. (2000). Methods used to teach social work students in the field: A research report from New Zealand. *Social Work Education, 19*(2), 145–154. doi:10.1080/02615470050003520

Matarazzo, R. G. (1978). Research on the teaching and learning of psychotherapeutic skills. In S. L. Garfield & A. E. Bergin (Eds.), *Handbook of psychotherapy and behavior change: An empirical analysis* (2nd ed., pp. 941–966). New York, NY: Wiley.

Mayer, R. E. (2004). Should there be a three-strikes rule against discovery learning? The case for guided methods of instructions. *American Psychologist, 59*(1), 14–19. doi:10.1037/0003-066X.59.1.14

McGaghie, W. C., Issenberg, S. B., Cohen, E. R., Barsuj, J. H., & Wayne, D. B. (2011). Does simulation-based medical education with deliberate practice yield better results than traditional clinical education? A meta-analytic comparative review of the evidence. *Academic Medicine, 86,* 706–711. doi:10.1097/ACM.0b013e318217e119

Miller, E., & Green, A. R. (2007). Student reflections on learning cross-cultural skills through a "cultural competence" OSCE. *Medical Teacher, 29*(4), e76–84.

Miller, M. (2004). Implementing standardized client education in a combined BSW and MSW program. *Journal of Social Work Education, 40*(1), 87–102. doi:10.1080/10437797.2004.10778481

Mossey, P. A., Newton, J. P., & Stirrups, D. R. (2001). Scope of the OSCE in the assessment of clinical skills in dentistry. *British Dental Journal, 190*(6), 323–326. doi:10.1038/sj.bdj.4800961

Munro, E. (2011). *The Munro review of child protection: Final report.* Retrieved from https://www.gov.uk/government/publications/munro-review-of-child-protection-final-report-a-child-centred-system

National Academy for Academic Leadership. (2013). *Assessment and evaluation in higher education: Some concepts and principles.* Retrieved from http://www.thenationalacademy.org/readings/assessandeval.html

Ndiwane, A., Omanand, K., & Theroux, R. (2014). Implementing standardized patients to teach cultural competency to graduate nursing students. *Clinical Simulation in Nursing, 10*(2), e87–e94. doi: 10.1016/j.ecns.2013.07.002

New Leadership Alliance for Student Learning and Accountability. (2012). *Committing to quality: Guidelines for assessment and accountability in higher education.* New York, NY: New Leadership Alliance for Student Learning and Accountability.

Powell, M. B., Fisher, R. P., & Hughes-Scholes, C. H. (2008). The effect of intra- versus post-interview feedback during simulated practice interviews about child abuse. *Child Abuse & Neglect, 32*(2), 213–227. doi:10.1016/j.chiabu.2007.08.002

Raskin, M. (1994). The Delphi study in field instruction revisited: Expert consensus on issues and research priorities. *Journal of Social Work Education, 30*(1), 75–88. doi:10.1080/10437797.1994.10672215

Rawlings, M. (2010). *Azusa Pacific University scale performance rating scale.* Azusa, CA: Azusa Pacific University.

Rawlings, M. (2012). Assessing BSW student direct practice skill using standardized clients and self-efficacy theory. *Journal of Social Work Education, 48*(3), 553–576. doi:10.5175/JSWE.2011.201000022

Rawlings, M., & Johnson, B. (2011). *Reliability and validity of the OSCE for Social Work Practice Performance Rating Scale.* Paper presented at the Council on Social Work Education Annual Program Meeting, Atlanta, GA.

Rawlings, M., & Johnson, B. (2012, November). *Predictive validity of student OSCE scores on field internship performance.* Poster presented at the Council on Social Work Education Annual Program Meeting, Washington, DC.

Regan, J. R. C., & Youn, E. J. (2008). Past, present, and future trends in teaching clinical social work skills through Web-based learning environments. *Journal of Social Work Education, 44*(2), 95–115.

Regehr, C., Bogo, M., Donovan, K., Anstice, S., & Kim, A. (2012). Identifying student competencies in macro practice: Articulating the practice wisdom of field instructors. *Journal of Social Work Education, 48*, 307–319. doi:10.5175/JSWE.2012.201000114

Regehr, C., Bogo, M., & Regehr, G. (2011). The development of an online practice-based evaluation tool. *Research in Social Work Practice, 21*(4), 469–475. doi:10.1177/1049731510395948

Regehr, G., Bogo, M., Regehr, C., & Power, R. (2007). Can we build a better mousetrap? Improving measures of social work practice performance in the field. *Journal of Social Work Education, 43*(2), 327–343. doi:10.5175/JSWE.2007.200600607

Regehr, G., MacRae, H., Reznick, R. K., & Szalay, D. (1998). Comparing the psychometric properties of checklists and global rating scales for assessing performance on an OSCE-format examination. *Academic Medicine, 73*(9), 993–997.

Reynolds, M., & Snell, R. (1988). *Contribution to development of management competence.* Sheffield, UK: Manpower Services Commission.

Rogers, G., & McDonald, P. L. (1995). Expedience over education: Teaching methods used by field instructors. *The Clinical Supervisor, 13*(2), 41–65. doi:10.1300/J001v13n02_04

Rogers, R. R. (2001). Reflection in higher education: A concept analysis. *Innovative Higher Education, 26*(1), 37–57. doi:10.1023/A:1010986404527

Ruch, G. (2007). Reflective practice in contemporary child care social work: The role of containment. *British Journal of Social Work, 37,* 659–680. doi:10.1093/bjsw/bch277

Schon, D. (1983). *The reflective practitioner: How professionals think in action.* London, UK: Temple Smith.

Schon, D. (1987). *Educating the reflective practitioner.* San Francisco, CA: Jossey-Bass.

Shulman, L. (2009). *The skills of helping individuals, families, groups, and communities* (6th ed.). Belmont, CA: Cengage Brooks/Cole.

Shulman, L. S. (2005). Signature pedagogies in the professions. *Daedalus, 134*(3), 52–59.

Simmons, B., Egan-Lee, E., Wagner, S. J., Esdaile, M., Baker, L., & Reeves, S. (2011). Assessment of interprofessional learning: the design of an interprofessional objective structured clinical examination (iOSCE) approach. *Journal of Interprofessional Care, 25*(1), 73–74. doi:10.3109/13561820.2010.483746

Social Work Reform Board (SWRB). (2010, September). Options paper: Progress report on developing a professional standards framework for social work. Retrieved from www.collegeofsocialwork.org/resources/reform-resources/

Soo, S., Berta, W., & Baker, G. R. (2009). Role of champions in the implementation of patient safety practice change. *Healthcare Quarterly, 12*(Special Issue), 123–128. doi:10.12927/hcq.2009.20979

Sowbel, L. R. (2011). Gatekeeping in field performance: Is grade inflation a given? *Journal of Social Work Education, 47*(2), 367–377. doi:10.5175/JSWE.2011.201000006

Sturpe, D. A. (2010). Objective structured clinical examinations in doctor of pharmacy programs in the United States. *American Journal of Pharmaceutical Education, 74*(8), 148–157. doi:10.5688/aj7408148

Sun, A. (1999). Issues BSW interns experience in their first semester's practicum. *The Clinical Supervisor, 18*(1), 105–123. doi:10.1300/J001v18n01_07

Suskie, L. (2009). *Assessing student learning: A common sense guide.* San Francisco, CA: Jossey-Bass.

Talbot, M. (2004). Monkey see, monkey do: A critique of the competency model in graduate medical education. *Medical Education, 38*(6), 587–592. doi:10.1046/j.1365-2923.2004.01794.x

Taylor, I. (1997). *Developing learning in professional education: Partnerships for practice.* Buckingham, England: Open University Press and Society for Research Into Higher Education.

Taylor, I., & Bogo, M. (2013). Perfect opportunity—perfect storm? Raising the standards of social work education in England. *British Journal of Social Work.* doi:10.1093/bjsw/bct077

Trumble, S. (2012). The reason for clinical simulation. *The Clinical Teacher, 9,* 273–274. doi:10.1111/j.1743-498X.2012.00639.x

Turner, J. L., & Dankoski, M. E. (2008). Objective structured clinical exams: A critical review. *Family Medicine, 40*(8), 589–591.

van der Vleuten, C. P. M., & Swanson, S. (1990). Assessment of clinical skills with standardized patients: State of the art. *Teaching and Learning in Medicine, 2,* 58–76. doi:10.1080/10401339009539432

Vinton, L., & Wilke, D. (2011). Leniency bias in evaluating clinical social work student interns. *Clinical Social Work Journal, 39*(3), 288–295. doi:10.1007 /s10615-009-0221-5

Watson, R., Stimpson, A., Topping, A., & Porock, D. (2002). Clinical competence assessment in cursing: A systematic review of the literature. *Journal of Advanced Nursing, 39*(5), 421–431. doi:10.1046/j.1365-2648.2002.02307.x

Wayne, J., Bogo, M., & Raskin, M. (2010). Field education as the signature pedagogy of social work education: Congruence and disparity. *Journal of Social Work Education, 46*(3), 327–339. doi:10.5175/JSWE.2010.200900043

Wayne, J., Bogo, M., & Raskin, M. (2015). Non-traditional field models. In C. Hunter, J. Moen, & M. Raskin (Eds.), *Foundations for excellence: Social work field directors* (pp. 41–59). Chicago, IL: Lyceum Books.

Weaver, A. (2011). High-fidelity patient simulation in nursing education: An integrative review. *Nursing Education Perspectives, 32*(1), 37–40. doi:10.5480/1536-5026-32.1.37

Weinert, F. E. (2001). Concept of competence: A conceptual clarification. In D. S. Rychen & L. H. Salganik (Eds.), *Defining and selecting key competencies* (pp. 45–66). Seattle, WA: Hogrefe & Huber.

Wessel, J., Williams, R., Finch, E., & Gemus, M. (2003). Reliability and validity of an objective structured clinical examination for physical therapy students. *Journal of Allied Health, 32*(4), 266–269.

Wilson, A. B., Brown, S., Wood, Z. B., & Farkas, K. J. (2013). Teaching direct practice skills using Web-based simulations: Home visiting in the virtual world. *Journal of Teaching in Social Work, 33,* 421–437. doi:10.1080/08841233 .2013.833578

Wodarski, J. S., Feit, M. D., & Green, K. (1995). Graduate social work education: A review of two decades of empirical research and considerations for the future. *Social Service Review, 69*(1), 108–130. doi:10.1086/604098

Ziv, A., Small, S. D., & Wolpe, P. R. (2000). Patient safety and simulation-based medical education. *Medical Teacher, 22*(5), 489–495. doi:10.1080/01421590050110777

Assessment: The act of measuring student learning, which involves gathering credible evidence of inputs, such as educational activities and outcomes (i.e., student performance) for the purpose of improving effectiveness of instruction and programs and demonstrating accountability (Banta, 2013). See also *formative assessment* and *summative assessment.*

Evaluation: The assignment of relative value to an assessment such as a grade or final mark as to the acceptability of performance as compared with a benchmark or scale.

Formative assessment: Data and feedback provided to improve teaching, learning, and performance over a course or a program of study.

Global rating item: A single item used as part of an assessment measure assessing the overall quality of the practice performance of the student.

Global rating scale: A measure of performance involving a series of continuous items on which the students' competence in an OSCE is rated by trained observers.

Metacompetency: Metacompetencies are intellectual and cognitive capacities, interpersonal abilities, and self-reflection. They are higher-order, overarching abilities and qualities that are of a different order and nature than procedural competencies or operational behaviors and skills. Metacompetencies may be related to people's ability to learn the specific role competencies of particular professions and to use discrete behaviors in a purposeful, integrated, and professional manner.

Objective structured clinical examination (OSCE): An assessment format used in the education and assessment of health-care professionals for which actors (as in human simulation) or mannequins (nonhuman simulation) portray clients in a clinical setting in a consistent and standardized manner for the purpose of assessing student competence. The original OSCE format involves a multistation examination in which students perform with a standardized patient in a timed interaction and are watched and rated by a faculty member before moving to the next station. Students are rated on a checklist or global rating scale.

Performance-based assessment: A form of testing in which the demonstration of clinical skills is observed to assess the practice competence of students or practitioners.

Pilot testing: Pretesting of an OSCE involving the standardized client, a volunteer student or experienced practitioner, and a rater, used as an opportunity to refine the case scenario, train the actor, and observe an OSCE as it would function in an examination to make necessary adjustments before its formal use.

Postencounter guided reflection (also known as a *reflective dialogue*): A form of reflection-based assessment involving questions administered to students immediately after a client interaction during an OSCE to elicit a range of underlying components of competence that affect students' performance in the interview. Some components are the students' conceptualization of social work practice, their ability to use their conceptualization of practice to inform their understanding of their performance, and their ability to use this informed understanding of their performance to imagine potential changes in both future performance and conceptualizations of practice. Self-awareness about emotional reactions and regulation can also be examined in a reflection.

Procedural competence: Skills and techniques that are demonstrated in the behavior of professionals as they carry out procedures in the domains associated with their profession. The EPAS framework refers to procedural competencies as practice behaviors.

Raters: Experienced practitioners or faculty members trained to observe and assess students' OSCE performances.

Reflection-based assessment: A form of assessment used to assess student meta-competencies, such as critical thinking, emotional regulation, and judgment.

Role play: The live acting out or performance of a particular scenario, usually used in training in human service professions. The role play is based on a script or can be fairly spontaneous. The role play provides student practitioners the opportunity for development and rehearsal of their practice skills. Students can also role play in relation to scenarios and simulated clients presented in segments on a video recording or in interaction with an avatar simulating a client.

Simulation: Guided experiences, often immersive, that replace or amplify real experiences. Simulation evokes or replicates substantial aspects of the real world in a fully safe, instructive, and interactive fashion (Gaba, 2007).

Standardized clients (also known as standardized patients): People who are trained to portray the full spectrum of characteristics of an assigned client role in a realistic and consistent manner that is reproducible from encounter to encounter. Used for the purposes of teaching and assessment.

Station: The vignette, rating scale, and location specification needed in the implementation of an OSCE. A multistation OSCE refers to multiple vignettes used in a series of performances to assess student performance.

Summative assessment: Data collected at the end of a course or program of study that involved the final assessment of what was learned.

Vignette (also known as a case scenario): Detailed information about the life of a client, including verbatim statements, description of client signs, symptoms, and characteristics, and positive and negative cues that provide guidelines for actor responses, which direct the performance of the standardized client.

OSCE for Social Work Practice Performance Rating Scale

Student Name: _____

Exam Instructor: _____

Integrated Social Work Knowledge, Values, and Skills Scale
(Integration of content and process dimensions)

As the student conducts the interview, examples of the following behaviors will reflect the student's level of performance on the dimensions to be examined.

- Appropriate use of open-ended questions

- Appropriate use of closed-ended questions

- Seeks clarification

- Seeks concreteness

- Active listening through demonstration of nonverbal behaviors (e.g., appropriate body posture, physical proximity, facial expression, encouragements such as head nods, attentive gaze)

- Active listening through demonstration of verbal behaviors (e.g., utterances and simple furthering comments, voice tone, speech rate, and volume)

- Restatement or paraphrase of content, thoughts, and meanings

- Reflection of feelings

- Appropriate use of silence

- Summary

Source: Bogo, Katz, Logie, Regehr, C. & Regehr, G. (Revised, 2012)

OSCE for Social Work
Practice Performance Rating Scale

Please circle the number corresponding to the candidate's performance. You may also write brief comments.

I. Develops and uses a collaborative relationship

Introduction				
1	2	3	4	5
Does not introduce self or role or agency service	Introduces self; no description of role or agency service	Before end of the interview introduces self and role but is general or vague about agency's service	Before end of the interview introduces self, role, and agency service	Sets the stage by introducing self, role in context of agency's service

Response to Client: general content and process (about communications and feelings)				
1	2	3	4	5
Inappropriate or no response to client's communications and feelings.	Responds to client with cognitive, behavioral or factual comments. No response to feelings expressed or implied.	Mainly task and event focused, with occasional warm and empathic response to client's feelings.	Frequent warm and empathic responses to client's concerns, expressed and implied feelings.	Consistent warm and empathic responses to client's concerns, expressed and implied feelings, and assists clients in putting feelings into words.

Response to Client: specific to situation (about death of husband, illness, accident, coming out youth, elderly, child protection)				
1	2	3	4	5
Does not provide realistic reassurance or support or makes negative comments	Occasional realistic reassurance and support on a mechanical level	Some realistic reassurance and support, not consistent, and sometimes mechanical	Consistent realistic reassurance and support with some empathic connection	Effective, consistent, and empathic, realistic reassurance and support

Focus of interview				
1	2	3	4	5
Interview has no coherence or rigidly follows student's own agenda	Minimal direction but still too focused on own agenda, and pace too fast or slow	Provides direction but moves too quickly or too slowly to change topic	Provides direction, pace more appropriate; some transitions are rough	Provides direction to the interview, maintaining focus, flow, and smooth transitions while remaining responsive to client concerns

II. Conducts an ecosystemic assessment

Presenting problem				
1	2	3	4	5
Does not address presenting problem, current situation, or precipitant event	Sole focus on presenting problem; does not identify current situation or precipitant event	Can identify presenting problem; gathers minimal info about current situation and precipitant event	After some time identifies presenting problem, precipitant event, and situation	Efficiently identifies present problem, situation, and precipitant with linkages between them

Systemic assessment: nuclear family, extended family, neighborhood, friends, employment, school				
1	2	3	4	5
Comprehensive systemic inquiry missing	Struggles to focus on more than one system	Identifies some of most obvious systems, but connections between them lacking	Able to identify all relevant systems and some connections between problem and systems	Complete systemic assessment with depth in linkages between them

Strengths				
1	2	3	4	5
Focus exclusively on problems and deficits with no attention to client strengths	Minimal inquiry about strengths; still mainly problem focused	Begins to explore client strengths the client has not presented; less focus on problem	More than beginning inquiry and exploration of strengths in a way client has not presented	Consistent and effective inquiry exploration and identification of strengths in a way client has not presented

III. Sets the stage for collaborative goal setting

Involves client				
1	2	3	4	5
Does not ask client what he or she needs	Tells client what he or she needs	Occasional inquiry about what client believes he or she needs; no exploration of client rationale	Inquires in directive manner about what client believes he or she needs; little exploration of client rationale	Collaborative, consistent, and effective inquiry about and exploration of what client believes he or she needs

IV. Demonstrates cultural competence related to culture/gender/race/sexual orientation/age-ability

1	2	3	4	5
Appears uncomfortable with cultural differences	Inconsistent recognition of cultural cues and issues; interest in and openness to cultural difference	Displays interest and comfort with exploration of cultural difference	Consistent recognition of obvious cultural issues; asks about, listens to, and explores some cultural issues	Demonstrates comfort in consistent, effective exploration of cultural cues and content for understanding; appreciate cultural identity

Overall Assessment of the Knowledge and Skills Demonstrated in the Interview

Based on your impression of the candidate's performance, this candidate demonstrated competence at the level of				
1	2	3	4	5
No initiative or response to components of relationship building and assessment, no organization or cohesion	Very beginning and inconsistent attempts to take initiative, assess and build relationship, inconsistent organization and cohesion	Some consistent initiative and response to some components of relationship building and assessment, consistent organization and cohesion	Most often consistent in response to most components of relationship building and assessment, integrated organization and cohesion	Effective, consistent, perceptive initiative in all components of relationship building and assessment, efficient organization and cohesion

Source: Bogo, Katz, Logie, Regehr, & Regehr (2012)

Reflection Questions After the Interview

You have just completed an interview with a standardized client. You now have up to 25 minutes to answer the following questions. You will be informed just before the time limit, and you will stop writing at the 25-minute mark. Answers should be succinct. When completed, print this file in the computer lab where you are answering these questions and immediately bring it to the exam instructor who observed your interview (place this copy in the box outside the instructor's door).*

Student Name: _____

Exam Instructor: _____

1. What were the main issues the client was dealing with?
2. What have you learned in the social work program that influenced your approach with the client in this interview?
3. Did issues related to diversity affect your approach with the client in this interview? Please give an example.
4. Can you think of any personal or professional experiences that influenced your understanding of this client?
5. In the interview, how did you feel, and how did you use these feelings?
6. What did you find the most challenging in this client, and what was your approach to dealing with this challenge?
7. What is your opinion of your performance in the interview with the client?
8. What do you think you learned from this interview?
9. How might this learning experience influence your approach to other clients?

*Note: Reflective questions can also be asked orally by the rater, with video or audio recordings used to document responses.

Source: Bogo & Katz (2012), adapted from Bogo, Mylopoulos, Katz, Logie, Regehr, C., & Regehr, G., 2009.

OSCE for Social Work Post-OSCE Reflection Rating Scale

Student Name: _____

Exam Instructor: _____

Please circle the number corresponding to the student's performance. You can write additional comments as well.

1. Identifies the main issues

Content		
Q.1 What were the main issues the client was dealing with?		
Does not identify the main issues.	Identifies some of the main issues.	Identifies most of the main issues.

1	2	3	4	5

2. Conceptualization of practice/use of knowledge

Content		
Q.2 How do participants theoretically conceptualize substantive issues (culture, diversity, mental and physical health, isolation, neglect) in the scenario and for their practice?		
Does not use theoretical concepts to understand the issues. Is descriptive in discussing the scenario and approach to practice.	Uses some theoretical concepts to understand and analyze the relevant issues in the scenario. Some link of concepts to approach to practice.	Uses multiple theoretical concepts to understand and analyze the relevant issues in the scenario and approach to practice.

1	2	3	4	5

Content		
Q.3 Diversity: How do participants conceptualize issues of culture and diversity in their practice?		
Seem unaware of diversity issues and their potential impact on the case.	Recognize the relevant diversity issues but are unable to effectively integrate them into their approach to the case.	Recognition of complexity in dealing with diversity issues. Dealing with diversity is integrated into practice.

1	2	3	4	5

Process				
Q.3 How does participants' past knowledge and experience affect their approach to the case?				
Seeks to inappropriately apply a past experience to understanding the current case.		Seeks to appropriately apply a past experience to understanding the current case.		Past knowledge is used as a starting point for exploration of the current case. Knowledge informs thinking about the case but does not bound thinking.
1	2	3	4	5

3. Self-regulation

Link between affect, cognition, and action				
Q.5 How do participants deal with their own reactions and operate in a purposeful and intentional manner to form a therapeutic relationship?				
Self-focused, preoccupied with own reactions. Does not effectively address client needs.		Aware of self but unable to use as a tool in building a relationship. Imbalance between focus on self and focus on client.		Use own reactions purposefully to develop a therapeutic relationship with the client. The focus on self is balanced with client needs.
1	2	3	4	5

Link between affect, cognition, and action				
Q.6 How are participants thinking and feeling about their level of knowledge and skill about the client situation and social work role and their ability to address client needs?				
Are unable to accurately assess ability to effectively address client needs.		Are inconsistent in ability to accurately assess own ability to effectively address client needs.		Are able to accurately assess ability to effectively address client needs.
1	2	3	4	5

4. Professional development

Learning				
Q.7 What do participants focus on and talk about regarding their performance in the OSCE?				
Focus on attributing performance to examination factors.		Self-assessment of performance particularly focused on their own reactions and emotions. Explore particular strengths and weaknesses of the performance.		Self-assessment of practice, emphasis on what they can take from this experience and apply to their practice. Reflective conceptualization of practice strengths and weaknesses.
1	2	3	4	5

Learning		
Q.8 What do participants focus on and talk about regarding their learning in the OSCE?		
Accrues facts about the case (e.g., patient issues, characteristics).	Identifies principles of practice that were in evidence in case.	Considers how current case informs broader practice.
1	2	3	4	5

Growth		
Q.9 What do participants say about how they would integrate this experience into their practice?		
Does not consider impact on practice.	Considers ways in which this experience could affect future performance with a similar client.	Emphasizes the role of each new experience in the process of continuous reformulation of practice.
1	2	3	4	5

Source: Bogo & Katz (2012); adapted from Bogo, Mylopoulos, Katz, Logie, Regehr, C., & Regehr, G., 2009.

Azusa Pacific University Performance Rating Scale

(Based on EPAS 2008 Competency 10 a and b, Council on Social Work Education)

EPAS 2.1.10 Competency: Engage, assess, intervene, and evaluate with individuals, families, groups, organizations, and communities.

Azusa Pacific University Student Learning Outcome 10: Apply knowledge and skills of generalist social work practice with individuals, families, groups, organizations, and communities.

10.a Engagement

Practice Behavior

a. Develops a collaborative working relationship				
1	2	3	4	5
Unable to develop connection with client, does not introduce self or role.		Sets foundation for working relationship, including introduction of self and agency.		Clear connection made with client, with clear introduction of self, role, and agency.

b. Demonstrates interviewing and interpersonal skills				
1	2	3	4	5
Interview has no coherence or direction or rigidly follows own agenda.		Demonstrates basic interviewing skills such as open-ended questions, warmth, and acceptance, may move too fast or slow in interview or relationship.		Excellent interviewing skill, with good pacing and direction, with attention to client feelings and relationship.

c. Demonstrates awareness of how perceived by clients and able to modify behavior as indicated by client response.				
1	2	3	4	5
No evidence of self-awareness or change in behavior in response to client.		Demonstrates insight into use of self and perceptive of client response.		Excellent awareness of client perception with advanced skill in appropriately modifying behavior.

d. Effectively prepares for meetings/interactions with clients				
1	2	3	4	5
No evidence of outside preparation for meeting.		Adequately prepared for client session.		Thorough preparation for meeting demonstrated.

10.b Assessment

Practice Behavior

a. Assess client systems, including strengths, limitations, risk factors, and cultural considerations.				
1	2	3	4	5
Minimal coverage of key client systems.		Key content areas addressed.		Comprehensive assessment, including all key content areas, risk factors, and cultural considerations.

b. Organize key content areas, including basic summary and interpretation of client data				
1	2	3	4	5
No clear summary or interpretation of data.		Able to provide basic summary for client and beginning interpretation of meaning of data.		Clear and comprehensive summary of data, with meaningful interpretation of data.

c. Develops mutually agreed upon goals and outcomes				
1	2	3	4	5
Sets goals for client, without client input, or does not clearly articulate goal.		Seeks client input in the development of goals and outcomes.		Goals clearly developed, with mutual input from social worker and client.

d. Selects appropriate intervention strategies based on assessment				
1	2	3	4	5
Intervention strategy not presented or strategy not related to assessment.		Able to use data from assessment to inform intervention strategy.		Clear linkages of assessment to intervention strategies, with clear articulation for client.

Overall rating				
1	2	3	4	5
Poor	Needs more training	Beginning level of skill (basic competency)	Good	Excellent

Post–Reflective Dialogue Questions and Comments:

_____

_____

_____

_____

Source: Rawlings (2010).

Supplemental Risk Assessment Scale Item

This risk assessment item can be added to either performance scale as applicable to case scenario and assessment goals.

Suicidality/abuse/competence				
1	2	3	4	5
Completely ignores risks presented by case.	Identifies risk but does not conduct risk assessment.	Identifies risk and conducts basic assessment.	Identifies risk, conducts thorough assessment, with beginning safety plan.	Correctly identifies risk, conducts thorough assessment, and initiates safety plan.

Source: Rawlings & Johnson (2011).

APPENDIX C
Case Scenarios

CASE SCENARIO: MRS. GONZALEZ
Instructions to Students

You are working as a school social worker for a local school board, and you cover four schools. Students and their families are referred to you by classroom teachers based on their concerns about students. Your role is to meet with families to assess for any psychosocial needs, to develop a plan for meeting those needs, and to connect families to resources to meet those needs. On average the school social worker can conduct a first interview and then meet with the family for up to four visits to complete an assessment and facilitate the referrals.

In this vignette you are meeting for the first time with a mother referred by her 13-year-old son's teacher. The son's grades have been dropping, and he has been acting out more in class. Your referral form indicates the mother's husband was killed 6 months ago in a car accident.

You will be meeting with the mother alone for the initial visit to assess what her needs are and to develop some initial goals. **This is the first 15 minutes of a 60-minute interview.**

Information for Standardized Client
I. Demographic Information

The client is a 42-year-old woman from Mexico, recently widowed, with three children aged 5, 7, and 13. She is coming to see the social worker after being referred by her son's teacher. The son has experienced a drop in grades and increased acting out in school. The teacher is aware of the recent death of the father and thought a school social worker might be able to provide some assistance to the family.

II. History of Presenting Problem

Tony is 13 and in grade 7. He has historically been an A and B student. Since the death of his father his grades have dropped to Ds and Fs. The mother has tried to encourage her son, but he no longer seems to care about his grades. Tony has been acting out for about 6 months. He has been in three fights and has been sent down to the office on three other occasions. He has been given detentions for his behavior. Tony recently skipped the last one, prompting a call from the teacher, who is worried about the changes she is observing. His mother needs him to pick up his two younger sisters (Angie and Sophie) from a neighboring school and take care of them until she gets home from work at about 6:30. Tony skipped the detention to do this. The other children have not experienced any change in their school status.

At home Tony is sullen and unhelpful, which is not like him. He watches TV and won't respond to requests to come for dinner or to help out with things his mother needs him to do.

The client has had to return to work full time since her husband's death to support the family and is worried about what will happen if Tony is unable to pick up his sisters. She is working as a nurse's aide in a geriatric facility (bathing, grooming, feeding, and walking seniors). This has been a significant change for the family, as before the mother stayed home. Now the mother must drop the children off very early before school and can't get home until 6:00 p.m. or sometimes 6:30 p.m. The girls stay in a "kid's club" at the school until Tony picks them up around 4 p.m. The mother is extremely worried about finances because each month she must dip into her husband's $40,000 life insurance policy to make the house payment, pay for child care, and so on. She fears what will happen when this money runs out. She has no family nearby, and a few friends, who she thinks are busy with their own families. Her sister and sister's family live an hour away, at the other end of the city. The mother's physical health is unremarkable except that she is not sleeping well, has little appetite, and is exhausted and worried about the effects of her working on the three children, especially Tony, who is taking the brunt of the extra work and is acting out. She is concerned that Tony, her male child, should not be doing so much housework. The children's health is good.

The client had been married to her husband for 15 years and reports they had a solid marriage where they both worked hard to make a better life for their family. Mr. Gonzalez worked in construction.

III. Emotional State

The client reports being frequently tearful and has difficulty sleeping. She is not eating very well and is frazzled. She is moderately depressed, without suicidal ideation. During the interview, the mother is anxious and expresses feeling overwhelmed with her new responsibilities and Tony's behavior. Eye contact is fair. The client is educated and articulate. Mrs. Gonzalez received no counseling after the death of her husband and went straight to work trying to keep the family afloat.

IV. Items to Be Used Verbatim by Client

- "I'm very worried about money. Every month I have to take money from the life insurance."
- "I'm feeling very overwhelmed, and I can tell I don't have as much patience with the kids."
- "In my own country this wouldn't be such a problem."
- "And Tony shouldn't have to take on these responsibilities; he is a boy."
- "I don't have any time to supervise homework as I used to."

V. Social Worker's Goals for Client (Mrs. Gonzalez)

The following are key issues that the student should explore. The actor should respond positively if the student does explore these key issues:

- Explore family's financial situation.
- Assess implications of father's death for son.
- Assess son's adjustment to father's death.
- Assist client in connecting to educational resources to address academic and social issues to avoid negative peer group influences.

- Help the client articulate and appreciate the various losses affecting her.
- Assess family situation.
- Assess effects of cultural issues as a result of immigration.

Source: This case was originally developed by Mary Rawlings and further developed for the OSCE for Social Work Project by Nancy McNaughton.

CASE VIGNETTE: MR. PHILLIPS

Instructions to Students

As a hospital social worker in a large, local hospital, you cover general medicine. Your role is to meet with families to

- Assess for any psychosocial needs.
- Develop a plan for meeting those needs.
- Connect patients and families to resources as needed to meet those needs.

On average the hospital social worker can conduct a first interview, usually conducted in a small office just outside the ward, and then meet with the family during the patient's hospital stay (the length varies depending on the issue, and the medical staff generally decides when discharge will occur) to complete an assessment and facilitate the referrals.

In this vignette, you are meeting for the first time with the patient, referred to social work by the nursing staff. The patient was in a car accident and broke a leg and an arm. There are medical investigations for possible internal injuries. Mr. Phillips is unable to work and is concerned about his financial situation and the family's financial security. Mr. Phillips is married and has two children, a daughter (age 12) and a son (age 9).

You will be meeting with the patient whenever you can catch him during your time on the hospital ward. **You will be conducting the first 15 minutes of a 45-minute interview with Mr. Phillips to get a sense of his current situation and psychosocial needs.**

Information for Standardized Client

I. Demographic Information

The patient is a 40-year-old man with a wife, aged 35 years, from a suburban community without the specialized facilities for treating complex medical conditions. The patient was transferred to this large teaching hospital, and his family remains in the outlying community. He earns a low salary. The couple has two children, a daughter (age 12) and a son (age 9).

II. History of Presenting Problem

John Phillips runs an office of three employees in a small tire company, Fountain Tire. His wife, Susan Phillips, is 35 and works as a law clerk in a suburban law office. The family lives in a small suburban community with no extended family. The extended family is spread out from coast to coast, with the family originally from the East Coast. The couple has been married for 15 years and live and work in a small town 50 miles from the hospital. The daughter, Elizabeth, is in grade 7 at a local middle school, and the son, David, is in grade 4 at the local elementary school.

John was injured in a car accident when, driving through an intersection, he was hit by another car. His car was not moving all that fast, but it still resulted in a broken left leg and left arm and potential internal injuries. He was not at fault. During the interview he is visibly in pain, wincing periodically. Before the accident, John's health was excellent and he was physically active. John has not investigated his benefits, and he is not certain about the coverage he has, when it begins, and the extent of the payments for any potential disability. He also does not know whether the family is covered for any at-home nursing care or is due any kind of payment for expenses such as a wheelchair or other assistive devices.

John and Susan have had a traditional marriage, although Susan has recently been the primary breadwinner. Susan and John met in high school and married soon after that. Susan did not work while going to college, and the couple incurred a large student loan debt. The children were born, and Susan remained at home with the children until David started grade 1. She began her position as a law clerk at that time to occupy herself once both children were gone all day. Although Susan's salary was a fairly recent addition to the family's income, it was being used to pay off her student loans. The couple had come to count on her salary since their move a year ago to a larger home with a larger mortgage.

With John's current health problems, the family routine has been severely disrupted. Susan is commuting to the hospital to be with John every day after work. The children must make their own way home and have not been able to attend any of their after-school activities. Elizabeth is left to care for David after school and to provide some kind of supervision over dinner. Dinner currently consists of prepared meals from the supermarket.

III. Emotional State

John is overwhelmed at the sudden upheaval and changes to the family's life. He exhibits a great deal of anxiety and finds it difficult to talk about the family situation. John has never been particularly articulate and has been overshadowed by his wife's education and profession. He is worried about losing his job and therefore eager to be released from hospital to return to work.

IV. Items to Be Used Verbatim by Client

- *Initial statement:* "I've talked to so many people. I hope you can help me because I don't need this right now."
- *Five-minute prompt:* "A man isn't a man unless he can work."
- "They pump me with meds. I don't know what I am on. I want to get off it. I don't mind the pain, and I want to be able to think straight."
- "I am worried about having to take time off from my job in case I lose it. I don't know if we can manage without my salary."
- "My wife is coming to the hospital every day and not spending time with the children. I don't know whether they can manage without her. It's not fair that their lives are totally changed right now."
- *Seasonal activity prompts:* Playing baseball in the summer, hockey in the winter.

V. Social Worker's Goals for Client (Mr. Phillips)

The following are key issues that the student should explore. The actor should respond positively if the student does explore these key issues.

- Get a sense of the family's financial situation.
- Short-term planning: Get a sense of immediate adjustment to current change in patient and its effect on the family.
- Long-term planning: Help client articulate his concern about potential long-term plan if he is suffering from internal injuries and must be off work for a prolonged time.

- Explore with client possible ways to discuss the family's situation with his wife and their children.

VI. Suggested Props

- Crutches
- Casts for arm and leg or sling for arm

Source: Case developed by Ellen Katz with additional input from Ilana Perlman.

CASE VIGNETTE: SIMONE

Instructions to Students

You are working as a social worker at a youth mental health agency. Youths are referred to you by families and schools and can also be self-referred. Your role is to meet with youths to assess for any psychosocial needs, to develop a plan for meeting those needs, to provide counseling, and to connect youths to resources to meet those needs. On average the youth social worker can conduct a first interview and then meet with the youth for up to 12 visits, to complete an assessment, provide counseling, and facilitate the referrals.

In this vignette, you are meeting for the first time with a 18-year-old woman who self-referred. Her grades have been dropping, and she has been experiencing anxiety and high levels of stress. Your referral form indicates that she attends high school and is in grade 12.

You will be meeting with Simone for the initial visit to assess what her needs are and to develop some initial goals. **This scenario is the first 15 minutes of a 60-minute session with the client.**

Information for Standardized Client

I. Demographic Information

The client is an 18-year-old Jamaican Canadian woman, in grade 12, attending a secondary school, Parkdale Collegiate. She is the middle child, with an older sister (Revlyn, 21 years old) and a younger brother (Brian, 15 years old). After several weeks of going to the school building in the morning but not attending classes, she was sent to the school counselor, who recommended that she self-refer to Youth Connections, a youth-focused mental health agency. She has experienced a drop in grades (from As to C+s), decreased appetite, and anxiety and has stopped hanging out with her friends.

II. History of Presenting Problem

Simone is 18 and in grade 12. She has historically been an A student. Since the beginning of the semester 2 months ago, Simone has been missing classes, has stopped hanging out with her friends, has stopped playing sports (soccer and basketball), and has been isolating herself in her room at home. She has been experiencing episodes of anxiety, has stopped eating regular meals, and has been feeling hopeless. Her parents are concerned, but she does not feel she can talk to them about her problems. Simone may dress in baggy clothing or may dress in more of a "girly" style.

Simone has been feeling very stressed out because she thinks she may be attracted to other girls at school. She started noticing her attraction to one of her close friends, Melissa, and was feeling worried that she might be gay or a lesbian. One particular incident occurred with Melissa. At a party, Melissa was drunk, and on a dare Melissa and Simone engaged in a kiss. Melissa has been reluctant to talk with Simone since that incident. Simone wonders what that incident was all about. She is terrified that anyone might find out about these feelings, especially her friends. When her friends are talking about boys they are interested in, she feels like she has nothing to say and has nobody to talk to about her feelings. Her friends joke about her needing to get a boyfriend, and she worries they will find out or suspect she might be a lesbian. So she has stopped hanging out with these friends and spends much time alone at home.

Simone knows that her church does not accept gay people, and she sees many of her close friends at church and is afraid to spend time with them as well. Simone is afraid to continue playing sports (soccer, basketball) because she is afraid she will feel attracted to other girls, and she does not want to feel these feelings. She is too worried of being rejected by her older sister, who has a boyfriend and is in college, to talk to her about her feelings.

III. Emotional State

Simone reports being frequently struck by anxiety and is feeling overwhelmed, especially about the incident with Melissa, and hopeless. She has difficulty sleeping. She is not eating regularly and has lost 5 pounds over the last 2 months. She is eating only cereal and toast, and when she is absorbed in her concerns she does not eat at all. When she has bouts of anxiety, she feels her heart start to race and feels nausea and trembling. During the interview, Simone is anxious and uncomfortable, with poor eye contact, and looks down at the ground a lot. She does not feel comfortable discussing questions about her sexuality, and she needs prompting to talk and reassurance that her feelings of attraction to other girls are okay and normal. Simone has never talked to anyone else before about these concerns about her sexual orientation.

IV. Items to Be Used Verbatim by Client

- "There's no one. No one gets me. I'm nowhere. I'm on my own."
- "When I am hanging around my friends, they are always talking about sex and trying to set me up."
- "People would hate me and never talk to me again."
- "I feel like I am going crazy with all of this."
- "I think being gay is not right, nasty, and sick."
- "If my parents ever found out about what happened at the party... ."

V. Social Worker's Goals for Client (Simone)

The following are key issues that the student should explore. The actor should respond positively if the student does explore these key issues.

- Assist client in articulating and appreciating that her feelings about her sexuality are normal.
- Explore her anxiety about going to school.
- Get a sense of her social interactions with her friends to potentially maintain them.
- Get a sense of her connections with family, sports, and church to potentially maintain them.
- Provide information about relevant resources.

Source: Case developed by Carmen Logie and Marion Bogo.

CASE VIGNETTE: MS. MARY PETERS

Instructions to Students: Version 1

In this vignette, you are meeting for the first time with a 75-year-old woman who self-referred. Although the older woman has been finding it increasingly difficult to leave home, she has come to the office to see you. Ms. Peters indicated to the intake worker that she has been feeling somewhat depressed lately because of her increasing frailty. The issue of confidentiality has already been dealt with, so there is no need for you to address the issue.

The agency is a community organization that serves older adults in the community experiencing physical or cognitive challenges. Older adults are referred to you, the social worker, by families and health-care professionals and can also be self-referred. Typically, clients are referred for services when they are experiencing some changes in their functioning. Your role is to meet with older adults to assess for any psychosocial needs, to develop a plan for meeting those needs, to connect older adults to resources to meet those needs, to provide some short-term counseling when indicated, and to monitor the client's adjustment over time. On average the community social worker can conduct a first interview, sometimes in the older adult's home and sometimes in the office, and then meet with the older adult and their family (if indicated) for as many visits as needed to ensure that the client's identified needs are being met. This interview is being conducted in the office.

You will be meeting with this older woman for an initial visit to assess what her needs are and to begin to develop some initial goals. **This is the first 15 minutes of a 60-minute session with the client.**

Instructions to Students: Version 2

The following is a simpler version of the instructions to students.

In this vignette, you are meeting for the first time with a 75-year-old woman who is self-referred. Although Ms. Peters has been finding it increasingly difficult to leave home, she has come to the office to see you. She indicated to the intake worker that she has been feeling somewhat depressed lately because of her increasing frailty as she becomes older. The issue of confidentiality has already been dealt with, so there is no need for you to address the issue.

The agency is a community organization that serves older adults in the community experiencing physical or cognitive challenges. These clients are referred to you, the social worker, by families, health-care professionals, or self-referral. Most typically, clients are referred for services when they are experiencing some changes in their lives. Your role is to meet with older adults to assess their psychosocial needs and to begin to develop an initial focus for the work in the context of a collaborative relationship.

This scenario is the first 15 minutes of a 60-minute session with the client.

Information for Standardized Client

I. Demographic Information

The client is a 75-year-old woman who currently lives alone. Ms. Mary Peters was never married and has no children. She is a retired school teacher (retired 10 years ago). She taught grade 5 at Wellesworth School. Ms. Mary Peters is the youngest of five siblings, only one of whom is still alive (Mr. John Peters, who is 79 years old and is married with two children). The other siblings are Paul (died of a stroke age 60, 21 years ago), and Dave (died of a heart attack at age 75, 3 years ago). Ms. Mary Peters' closest sibling, her sister, Anne Peters, died of colon cancer a year ago. The two women lived together all their lives because neither left home to get married. Ms. Mary Peters called the community organization because she has found it increasingly difficult to go out and is also feeling depressed and socially isolated.

II. History of Presenting Problem

Ms. Mary Peters' relationship with her only living sibling has been strained since her parents' death 20 years ago. Because Mary and Anne were both single, their families expected them to care for their aging parents, which they found quite burdensome at times. In the final years of their lives their parents recognized their daughters' sacrifices and decided to leave them the family home to ensure their financial security and to reward them for their years of caregiving. This generated a great deal of resentment among the other siblings.

Ms. Mary Peters has historically been a very healthy and active senior who participated in many weekly activities such as bridge and a knitting club. She began to attend these activities less frequently when her sister, Ms. Anne Peters, was diagnosed with cancer. Instead she spent her time attending doctor's appointments with her sister and providing her sister with a lot of emotional support. Ms. Mary Peters never resumed her social activities after her sister's death a year ago. Initially this was because she had typically attended these activities with her sister and could not bear attending them alone. Most recently, however, Ms. Mary Peters has found it challenging to leave the house because her arthritis has begun to affect her walking and has been causing her a great deal of pain. Ms. Mary Peters is beginning to feel depressed and isolated.

Ms. Mary Peters is quite worried about her emotional and physical health. She misses her sister terribly and finds that her arthritis, located in her hips, back, and knees, makes her feel "old and useless." She has lost contact with most of her friends and doesn't have anyone to talk to about her feelings. She is not on speaking terms with her only surviving sibling because he is still bitter that she and her sister inherited the family home. She is having trouble doing her grocery shopping and housework and fears that she may eventually have to leave the only home she has ever known. She last saw her doctor a few months ago after a fall. She does not want to go out to see her doctor often because this involves taking a taxi.

III. Emotional State

Ms. Mary Peters is feeling very sad and lonely. She is extremely thankful that the social worker has been able to see her because she has not had company for many months. She is very open about her emotions but is feeling hopeless about her situation.

IV. Items to Be Used Verbatim by Client

- *Initial statement (said struggling to get up to greet the social worker who is walking into the room):* "I'm so glad to see you. I've had a difficult time getting here this morning. Getting around is hard, and I never take a taxi."
- "It's terrible getting old."

- "I am used to being the one who cares for others."
- "I can't attend those terrible programs for old people; they are so depressing."
- "I'm all alone in the world."
- "I am finding it much harder to get around with my arthritis."
- "I'm not sure I can continue to manage with my arthritis."
- At the halfway mark, about 7 minutes into the interview, an unexpected moment that may pertain to a comment by the client in relation to her sister's death: "I miss her so much," said with great expression, perhaps tears.

V. Social Worker's Goals for Client (Ms. Mary Peters)

The following are key issues that the student should explore. The actor should respond positively if the student does explore these key issues.

- Help the client articulate and appreciate the various losses affecting her.
- Assess the family situation.
- Assess whether the client wants to reconnect to social activities that she finds meaningful (this is a long-term goal but can be initially discussed by understanding what activities Ms. Mary Peters finds meaningful) and assist her in taking steps to make these reconnections.
- Get a sense of the extent to which the client is struggling with activities of daily living to ensure that she can remain living safely independently.
- Work with issues of self-identity, including the client's negative feelings about aging.

Source: Case developed by Tamara Sussman and modified by Ellen Katz.

CASE VIGNETTE: NATALYA PETROVICH

Instructions to Students: Version 1

In this vignette you are meeting for the first time with a 26-year-old woman who self-referred. She has not been sleeping well at night. Your referral form indicates she is married, with one child, and not currently working outside the home. She has come to see you in the office and has left the baby in the child care area specifically for clients of the counseling center.

This is a community counseling center for newcomers to Canada. Clients are referred to you by families and doctors and can also be self-referred. Your role as a social worker is to meet with the client to assess for any psychosocial needs, to develop a focus for the work based on the assessed psychosocial needs, to provide counseling, and to connect clients to resources to meet those needs. On average the social worker can conduct a first interview and then meet with the client for up to seven visits, to complete an assessment, provide counseling, and facilitate any referrals.

You will be meeting with the client to assess what her needs are and to begin to develop an initial focus for the work. The issue of confidentiality has already been dealt with, so there is no need for you to address the issue. **This scenario is the first 15 minutes of a 60-minute session with the client.**

Instructions to Students: Version 2

The following is a simpler version of the instructions to students.

In this vignette, you are meeting for the first time with a 26-year-old woman who self-referred. She has not been sleeping well at night. Your referral form indicates she is married, with one child, and not currently working outside the home. She has come to see you in the office and has left the baby in the child care area specifically for clients of the counseling center.

This is a community counseling center for newcomers to Canada. Clients are referred to you by families or doctors and can also be self-referred. Your role as a social worker is to meet with the client to assess what her psychosocial needs are and to begin to develop an initial focus for the work in the context of a collaborative relationship. The issue of confidentiality has already been dealt with, so there is no need for you to address the issue. **This scenario is the first 15 minutes of a 60-minute session with the client.**

Information for Standardized Client

I. Demographic Information

The client is a 26-year-old Russian Canadian woman with a high school education who immigrated to Canada approximately 20 months ago with her husband of 4 years, Ivan, in search of a better life. Their families continue to reside in Russia and are of lower socioeconomic status. Natalya worked as a clerk in Walmart until she gave birth 3 months ago to a baby girl named Nora. She has not worked since giving birth. Natalya has a secondary school education.

II. History of Presenting Problem

Natalya is a 26-year-old woman who worked as a store clerk in Russia before immigrating to Canada 20 months ago. Both she and her husband are permanent residents. She and her husband are currently trying to help her parents, Iosif and Mariya, and three younger siblings immigrate to Canada but are finding the process lengthy, expensive, and time-consuming. She was employed at Walmart on a part-time basis and taking English classes when she became pregnant. The pregnancy was unplanned because Natalya and Ivan were saving all of their earnings to bring Natalya's family to Canada. Natalya stopped working after the baby was born to care for her infant. Because she did not have the requisite hours for unemployment insurance, she currently has no income. Her husband continues to work full-time in construction as a bricklayer, but since the birth he has supplemented their income with a part-time job as a waiter in a restaurant. Consequently, he works both days and evenings and is limited in the time he can spend with Natalya and the baby.

The pregnancy was unremarkable, and Natalya's daughter, now 3 months old, is healthy and thriving. Natalya's mother, Mariya, came from Russia on a short-term visitor's visa to help Natalya with the transition to motherhood but had to return home after a 6-week stay. Natalya reports receiving one visit from a public health nurse shortly after the baby was born and attends all medical appointments regularly but has had no other help with the baby. The baby is not yet sleeping through the night, and Natalya is feeling more and more fatigued and overwhelmed since her mother returned to Russia. She describes her doctor as "pleasant" but always in a rush and would not feel comfortable telling him how overwhelmed she is feeling.

Natalya and her husband live in a high-rise apartment building in the Parkdale area, and she does not know anyone else in the building. They do not attend religious services, because there is no Russian church in their area. Natalya has had little time to investigate community centers. Because her husband works so much, Natalya must care for her child, clean their apartment, and tend to her own needs.

III. Emotional State

Natalya reports feeling overwhelmed, hopeless, and anxious about the baby. Her sleeping and eating are sporadic, her appetite is diminished, and she has lost weight, which is a concern because she is breastfeeding. She is alone all the time and appears very fatigued. Natalya has not discussed this with anyone else. She is described as having a low mood.

IV. Items to Be Used Verbatim by Client

- *Opening statement:* "I feel overwhelmed, and there's no one to help me."
- "Sometimes I feel like leaving the apartment by myself and going away for a couple of hours."
- "I wish my mother were still here."
- "I can't do this."
- "I worry that I am not a good mother."
- At the halfway mark, about 7 minutes into the interview: unexpected moment that may pertain to frustration with the system.

V. Social Worker's Goals for Client (Natalya Petrovich)

The following are key issues that the student should explore. The actor should respond positively if the student does explore these key issues.

- Help client articulate her feelings of being overwhelmed by a new baby.
- Assess any concerns for the baby's safety and mother's potential to need assistance from child protection services.
- Assist client in articulating issues of self-identity in transition to motherhood.
- Assess social isolation and assist client in connecting to resources where she can meet others and obtain respite.

Source: Case developed by Lea Tufford and modified by Ellen Katz.

CASE SCENARIO: RUTH SMITH

Instructions to Students

You are a social worker for a program that serves older adults in the community. Your agency takes referrals from health-care professionals, families, Adult Protective Services, or self-referrals. The goal of your agency is to promote physical, emotional, social, and spiritual health of your clients. Clients are referred when changes in their health negatively affect their functioning.

Your role is to meet with the client for an initial interview to conduct a psychosocial assessment, to develop an initial plan for meeting any identified needs, and to connect your client to available resources. Your agency provides ongoing case management services as needed, with follow-up overtime, but does not provide traditional counseling services. Typically, the first interview is conducted in the person's home, or in the office, with a follow-up visit to the person's home at the next visit.

In this scenario, you are meeting with Ruth Smith, a 78-year-old woman brought to the agency by her daughter. The daughter is not participating in this initial interview because she had to pick up her own daughter from school. The referral sheet shows that the daughter has expressed concern about her mother's forgetfulness and her ability to stay safely living independently in her home, and it indicates that Ruth has been widowed for 5 years. **You will be conducting the first 15 minutes of what is typically a 30-minute initial visit.**

Information for Standardized Client

I. Demographic Information

The client is a 78-year-old Caucasian woman from a suburban neighborhood. She has been a widow for the last 5 years, living on her own in her home, which she owns. She presents as neat and clean. She has three children, all married—two daughters (Emily, 45, and Samantha, 50) and one son (John, 48)—and she has six grandchildren. Samantha and John both live out of state, one in Arizona and one in Texas. Emily lives close by and is the one who provides the primary caretaking for her mother. Emily has three children, ages 8–14 years old, and she works full time in a human resources position. Ruth had two older brothers, both of whom are deceased, with their widows still living in Oklahoma.

II. History of Presenting Problem

Ruth Smith was referred by her daughter Emily to Senior Care Support Services Network. Emily is becoming increasingly worried about Ruth's ability to live alone in her house. Emily reports that Ruth is becoming increasingly forgetful. For example, when Emily calls, Ruth has difficulty recalling what she had for dinner, if anything. Emily reports that Ruth is attending church less, whereas she used to go regularly, and that her house is not tidy. Emily reports that her mother has always been an excellent cook and that more and more her recipes are "off." Emily says she has been noticing little things like this more and more over the last year.

Although Emily is very supportive and assists her mother, she feels unable to have her move in with her in her home, which is already full with her family. She feels bad about this but doesn't know what else to do. She tries to stop by once a week but does miss weeks because of the busy schedule of her children. She has a primarily positive relationship with her mother, but at times she resents that her other siblings aren't more helpful.

Ruth had been married to her husband Gregory for 50 years, until Gregory's death from emphysema 5 years ago. She was born, raised, and married in Oklahoma. She and Gregory moved out to California in mid-1950s, seeking better job opportunities. Since his death, Ruth has generally coped well and kept close ties with her church, Monrovia Lutheran Church, but does miss him. Until recently, she was active in missionary circles and in helping in the church library. She has not been to church in 4 weeks. Ruth has not been employed since before her children were born. Gregory worked for the gas company and has a pension of about $450 per month, and about $680 from Social Security. Though on a fixed income, Ruth is financially stable and has Medi-Care and Medi-Cal. Ruth has never been to a senior center.

Generally Ruth is in good health, with no chronic health conditions other than some slight arthritis in her hands, and she finds reading more difficult. She has not had a physical in about a year and has not had her hearing checked. Current medicine is extra-strength Tylenol for the arthritis from the drug store. She tends to skimp on meals, relying on fruit, cereal, or other easy, quick food. Although her daughter worries about Alzheimer's disease, Ruth is showing only normal signs of aging.

She has become more hesitant to drive and therefore has not been leaving the house much. She had a fender bender about 6 months ago, which has shaken her confidence in driving and made her more isolated.

III. Emotional State

Ruth is very pleasant and sweet in the interview but somewhat resistant to help. She has been very independent her whole life and doesn't want to burden anyone. She is not depressed but is starting to withdraw more because of difficulties with driving, and fewer friends live close by. She also presents as hard of hearing, leaning forward to hear and asking the interviewer to speak up. She is somewhat private in the interview and tries to ask questions of the interviewer rather than to answer them.

IV. Items to Be Used Verbatim by Client

- "I don't know why I'm here. My daughter just worries about me for no reason."
- "I'm fine, honey, I am just 78 years old."
- "I feel like she wants me to move, but I've lived in this house 40 years, and I'm not moving."
- "I really don't like to drive anymore. I just go to the store and back, or church."
- "I don't cook much anymore. I mostly eat some fruit in the morning or whatever is easy and quick."
- "I would really like to get back to church."

V. Social Work Goals for Client Smith

Short term:

- Make linkages for medical checkup, with assessment for hearing.
- Assess psychosocial needs (e.g., activities of daily living, emotion, nutrition).
- Introduce linkages to transportation.

Long term:

- Increase social opportunities, whether reconnecting with church or other meaningful social activity.
- Maintain independent living status with supports.

Source: Case developed by Mary Rawlings with input from Barbara Johnson.

CASE SCENARIO: MR. HONG WU

Instruction to Students

You are working as a hospital social worker in a small community hospital. You are one of two social workers, and your role is to provide a range of social services, including discharge planning, family intervention, and risk assessment for suicide, domestic violence, and child abuse. You meet with clients anywhere from 15 minutes to 2 hours, depending on the needs of the client. You may meet once or multiple times, again depending on the need.

In this case, the doctor has made the referral to social services for you to assess a patient who was brought in the day before for a suicide attempt. He has been medically cleared for discharge, but they want you to assess his current level of suicidality and to link him to community resources, including a psychiatrist. The hospital chart indicates that the client took a handful of Tylenol after a breakup with a girlfriend. The chart states that the client is a Chinese man, 20 years old, currently attending a local college. He has been in the United States for only 18 months. He has insurance through the college student program.

You will be conducting the first 15 minutes of a 30-minute scheduled interview. After the interview, your instructor will ask you some follow-up reflective questions.

Information for Standardized Client

I. Demographic Information

The client is a 20-year-old Chinese student attending a local liberal arts college. He is just beginning his sophomore year. He came as a freshman from China to attend school. His parents are still in China, and they do not speak English. He has no siblings. His English is good. He has been medically cleared for discharge from the hospital; they have called you in as the social worker to assess his suicidality and to link him to community resources for follow-up.

II. History of Presenting Problem

Mr. Wu was brought into the hospital emergency room by his college roommates, who found him in his room unresponsive. Roommates report he had recently broken up with his girlfriend. Mr. Wu reported ingesting Tylenol, stating he just wanted to get some sleep and lost track of how many he took. (Lab shows high quantity but not lethal dose.) When asked how many, he replies, "Lost count." He reports being upset after the breakup with a girlfriend after 6 months. This was his first girlfriend. He denies suicidal intent and states he has never attempted suicide before, and he seems somewhat surprised that he did and is currently in the hospital. He is denying any suicidal ideation and just reports being really upset in that moment. He reports no family history of depression. Although reluctant, he does not decline outpatient follow-up but is resistant to inpatient psychiatric care.

Mr. Wu is doing well in school and has not experienced a drop in grades. He reports getting As and Bs and has a job on campus. He is isolated at school, and his girlfriend was his primary social contact. He is a math major. He lives in campus housing with two other students. They have a sociable but not close relationship. He does have friends in China that he keeps in contact with through Facebook and Skype. He has health insurance through the college student program.

Mr. Wu has had only limited contact with his family since coming to the United States, and he has not been back to China since he came. His father is an engineer, and his mother works in a factory. They are paying the majority of his school costs. He reports not being close with his family. They wanted him to come to the United States to study. He came at their urging. But he reports wanting to stay in the United States and finish school and does not want his parents contacted.

Mr. Wu does have symptoms of depression in that he reports difficulty sleeping and mostly staying in his room, isolating himself. He reports no prior incidents of depression, however. The treating doctor is recommending antidepressants but wants an outside psychiatrist to start and follow the medication. He has not been on medication previously. He has a car. He is open to talking to someone but expresses difficulty talking with Caucasians because of their cultural differences. He would prefer a Chinese doctor.

Client reports being Buddhist and denies use of alcohol or drugs.

III. Emotional State

Mr. Wu has good insight, seems embarrassed by what happened, and just wants to get out of the hospital and back to school. He is somewhat resistant to intervention but polite, with depressed demeanor, and is isolated at school. He makes little to no eye contact and uses a low, soft voice.

IV. Items to Be Used Verbatim by Client

- "Can you help me get out of here? I need to get back to school."
- "It was a stupid thing to do. I was just feeling really upset."
- "I'm having a hard time sleeping."
- "When I'm in China, I don't even realize I'm Asian. Only here do I realize it, because here they always put you in a group."

V. Social Worker's Goals for Client

- Assess current level of suicidality and determine whether the client is ready for discharge.
- Link the client to a psychiatrist and follow-up counseling.
- Increase social supports over the long term.

Source: Case developed by Mary Rawlings.

APPENDIX D
Course Material

SOCIAL WORK PRACTICE LABORATORY
Masters of Social Work Program
Factor–Inwentash Faculty of Social Work, University of Toronto

Final Assignment

On November 27, 2013, and November 28, 2013, students will conduct a standard interview as part of the evaluation of their learning in the course (SWK 4105). Just before the interview, students will be provided with a written case scenario and given 2 minutes to read it. This will prepare students for the interview. Students will then carry out the first 15 minutes of an interview with one of several standardized clients, played by an actor trained for the particular role. After the interview, the client will provide immediate brief feedback to the student as will the rater. The student will be rated by one of the SWK 4105 course instructors but not by their own course instructor.

Immediately after their interview and the feedback, students will spend approximately 25 minutes in the computer lab, where they will answer a set of questions designed to foster reflection on the just-completed interview. Each student will print out one copy of his or her responses and place it in a box outside the interview room. The instructor who observed the interview will rate the student's reflections and then forward the student's reflections and the rating scales to the student's course instructor, who will incorporate this information in written feedback to students as part of their overall evaluation in this course.

Specific Instructions for Students

One week before the OSCE students will receive the name and room number of the instructor who will be observing the OSCE and the date and time of the OSCE.

- Arrive at least 10 minutes before the scheduled time. It is critical that all interviews start exactly on time.
- Students are greeted in a designated room and given three labels with their name, their course instructor's name, and the name and room number of the OSCE rater.
- Students remain in the designated room until it is time to proceed with the OSCE.
- Students are seated outside the rater's room.
- Students will be provided with a written case scenario and given 2 minutes to read it.
- Students will conduct an interview (15 minutes).
- Students will receive brief feedback from the "client" and the rater for no longer than 5 minutes.
- Students will go to the computer lab immediately.
- Students have 25 minutes to answer the reflective questions.
- Students will print their answers to the reflective questions.
- Students will place these answers in a box outside the exam rater's room.
- Students will receive written feedback for overall performance in this course from their course instructor.

Source: Developed by Marion Bogo, Ellen Katz, and Andrea Litvack, Factor–Inwentash Faculty of Social Work.

SOCIAL WORK PRACTICE I
Bachelor of Social Work Program
Azusa Pacific University

Term Project

The goal of this assignment is to have the student demonstrate social work practice and interviewing skills in a role play situation using a standardized client (an actor trained to play the role of a client). It seeks to have students integrate such practice behaviors as self-awareness, gender considerations, and the effects of ethnicity and culture.

Assignment

You will be conducting an initial interview with a standardized client. Your role is one of a case manager, and you are meeting with your client for the first time to conduct an initial assessment and to develop initial intervention goals. This situation is designed to simulate as much as possible a role you may encounter in your internship so that you can demonstrate skills learned in the course. You will have 15 minutes to complete the interview. A bell will ring when you have 4 minutes left, and when your time is up a final bell will ring. When the final bell rings, your client will end the meeting and leave the room. Your professor will then ask you some follow-up questions so that you can explain your reasoning related to your approach and your next steps, as we realize that in 15 minutes you may not have had the chance to address everything that you are thinking about. During your interview your skills will be assessed by the professor in the room as an observer. Your interview will also be videotaped so that you can conduct a self-assessment of your skills. We understand that this can be anxiety provoking, but we believe it is the best way for the professor to give you specific feedback on your performance and for you to meet learning objectives of the course. Past students have highly praised the experience.

Procedure

1. Sign up for a time to conduct your interview.
2. Review the vignette and practice with friends and in class.
3. Arrive 15 minutes before your interview at your assigned time. Be on time. If you are late, you will forfeit your time. The professor will tell you when it is time to begin.
4. Enter the room and begin with your client.
5. End at the bell and remain in the room for follow-up questions.
6. After your follow-up questions have been completed, you are free to go.
7. The professor will then return to you a copy of your taped interview.
8. Write your self-evaluation and turn in on date of final.

Self-Evaluation

The second part of the assignment is a four-page, double-spaced, typed paper critiquing your skills. Include a brief description of how the problem-solving model can be applied in this case. Finally, reflect on your personal experience in the role of a clinician.

Grading:

- 70% faculty assessment of skills
- 30% self-reflection paper

MINDFULNESS THERAPY:
USING MINDFULNESS IN CLINICAL PRACTICE
Masters of Social Work Program
Factor–Inwentash Faculty of Social Work, University of Toronto

Process Recording and Reflection Exercise 2 After Simulation

This assignment will allow you to work in greater depth with your own clinical work, your attention, and your reflective processes. The purpose of the assignment is to assist you in continuing to build your level of competence, specifically in using mindfulness in clinical practice. The assignment is based on clinical skill and is not a term paper.

You will have your DVD of your 15-minute simulated interview. Using the three-part session intervention (1) psycho-education, (2) work with the bodymind, and (3) work with difficult emotions/emotional patterns, choose segments of your DVD simulation where you make use of this intervention. You want to be able to demonstrate the use of each of the three parts as per the chart below. These may be mindfulness-informed or mindfulness-based or a combination of the two. Transcribe material from each of these three parts for a total of about 5 minutes of the session. Then use the following table to reflect further on the specific components of each of the three parts of the session by listing (a) the mindfulness competencies used and the indicators (i.e., what you concretely did, such as the micro skills of tracking, contacting, and using directed mindfulness) that demonstrate that you indeed used those competencies and (b) the reason for your choice of competencies plus citations of literature that support your use of those competencies. In the final column, reflect on whether what you did was useful for the client or whether you would take different action if you could do the interview again. The assignment is to be no less than 5 pages and no longer than 10 pages. Each student will be assigned a time during the last week of classes to meet individually with the course instructor to review the DVD and the written assignment. The purpose of this final meeting is to have a dialogue about the simulated interview and the two assignments (Reflection 1 and Process Recording/Reflection 2). A final grade will be assigned after that final meeting.

Transcript	Phase of 3-part session	Mindfulness competencies used and indicators of those competencies	Reason for using specific competencies and citations of literature that support your use of the competencies	Reflection on your action; what you would do the same; what you would do differently next time
	Psycho-education			
	Work with the bodymind			
	Work with difficult emotions/ emotional patterns			

Reflection Exercise 1 After Simulation

Please answer the following five questions, taking no more than one page to answer each question. Your final submission should be no longer than five pages. The course instructor will not read more than one page for each answer.

Question 1 (Emphasis on the Bodymind and Prereflective Processing)

Reflect on the just-completed simulation in the same way you reflect on the weekly reading, by answering the following questions, based on the four foundations (or processes) of mindfulness:

a. What did I feel in the body (physical experience based on the posture, activities, and breath as related to the body)?

b. What was the emotion and accompanying emotional tone (the specific emotion you were experiencing and whether it was pleasant, unpleasant, or neutral)?

c. What was the state that I observed to be present in the mind (were any of the three poisons (anger, greed, ignorance) present; was the mind concentrated or distracted; was it heavy, sleepy, energetic, light, spacious, clear, clogged)?

d. What objects or thoughts were present in the mind (what were the concrete thoughts on which your feelings and state of mind were focused)?

Simply report what you observe; don't evaluate or analyze what you observe.

Question 2 (emphasis on cognitive reflection)
a. What was the effect of your affective state during the simulation on how you conducted the interview?
b. Reflecting on Question 1 and your answer to Question 2a, how would you manage your affective state differently in the future?

Question 3 (Mindfulness as Worldview and Reality, i.e., Ontology and Epistemology)
How do you use concepts from class readings and discussions of mindfulness philosophy and psychology to conceptualize the client's issues from the standpoint of mindfulness? *(I want to know how you understand the issues the client was dealing with from the standpoint of mindfulness. You do not need to reference any of our discussions or readings. But I want to know that you can integrate the philosophy and psychology of mindfulness into how you understand your clients.)*

Question 4 (Intervention)
How did you implement assessment, case conceptualization, and intervention concepts from class into your work with the client? *(I want to hear you discuss your assessment and intervention from our clinical discussions of using mindfulness in your clinical work. This way, I will know that you can employ the unique interventions offered by mindfulness as clinical theory to your work with clients in sessions.)*

Question 5 (Intervention)
How did you implement the three-part session (psycho-education, work with the bodymind, and work with difficult emotions and emotional patterns) in your work with the client?

Source: Developed by Ellen Katz.

Social Work Practice Laboratory Course SWK 4105: Final Feedback
Student Name:
Instructor Name:
Overall feedback comments:
Role play in classes.
DVD assignment.
Summary of OSCE rating and reflection.
Learning goals for the practicum:
Grade for the Course:

APPENDIX E
Forms for Conducting the OSCE

Instructions for OSCE Raters
For Instructors in Their Role as Raters

- Observe and rate nine interviews (or other designated number of interviews) each of the 2 days. Narrative and qualitative comments are important on performance and reflection rating scales.
- Each interview is 15 minutes in length.

Procedures

1. The rater will be seated in the interview room with the standardized client.
2. At the designated time the rater will greet the student, who is sitting outside the room.
3. The rater will provide students with a written case scenario.
4. The rater will receive from the student two labels. One will be placed on the Performance Scale and the other on the Reflection Scale.
5. Students have 3 minutes to read the case scenario.
6. Students are signaled to enter the room.
7. Students will conduct an interview (15 minutes).
8. Students will receive brief feedback from the "client" (2 minutes) and the rater (3 minutes) for a maximum of 5 minutes in total.
9. Complete the performance rating scale; maximum time needed is 5 minutes.
10. Take the written case scenario from the student; student is not to leave the room with the case scenario.

11. Periodically during the day you will receive the written reflections of the students you have observed and rated. (Students have 25 minutes to complete their reflections on the computer.) Student by student, read and rate the reflections using the reflection rating scale.

12. For each student, put together the performance rating scale, the student's written reflection, and the reflection rating scale.

13. Give the completed forms to the OSCE coordinator, who will put them in the student's course instructor's mailbox.

14. All ratings must be given to the OSCE coordinator by the end of the day.

15. Each instructor will receive the completed rating forms and reflections of the students in their own section.

16. Ratings on these forms will be integrated into your Final Evaluation Feedback and Grade (CR/NCR) for the Social Work Practice Laboratory Course.

OSCE Daily Interview Schedule: An Example

Actors to arrive at 9:00 a.m., Room 414.

Instructor and Rater Schedule: Interview Times	
Morning slot: 9:30 a.m. to 12:30 p.m.	**Afternoon slot: 1:30 to 4 p.m.**
9:30 First interview	1:30 Sixth interview
10:00 Second interview	2:00 Seventh interview
10:30 Third interview	*2:30 break*
11:00 break	3:00 Eighth interview
11:30 Fourth interview	3:30 Ninth interview
Noon Fifth interview	4:00 Tenth interview
12:30 lunch	4:30 End of day

Standardized Client Name	Vignette	Room #	Time	Rater
Christine E	Mary Peters	321	9:30	A
Christine E	Mary Peters	321	10:00	A
Christine E	Mary Peters	321	10:30	A
Break			*11:00*	
Christine E	Mary Peters	332	11:30	B
Christine E	Mary Peters	332	12:00	B
Lunch break			*12:30*	
Christine E	Mary Peters	352	1:30	C
Individual break			*2:00*	
Break			*2:30*	
Christine E	Mary Peters	336	3:00	D
Christine E	Mary Peters	336	3:30	D
Christine E	Mary Peters	336	4:00	D

OSCE for Social Work Student Feedback Form

Please circle the number that best describes your experience:

1. I think the standardized client was an effective way to assess my ability to practice social work skills with a client.

1	2	3	4	5
Strongly Disagree				Strongly Agree

2. The standardized client provided me with an opportunity to test my ability to integrate knowledge from theory and practice classes into an encounter with a client.

1	2	3	4	5
Strongly Disagree				Strongly Agree

3. I think the feedback provided through the standardized client will be effective in helping me improve my social work skills.

1	2	3	4	5
Strongly Disagree				Strongly Agree

4. I think using the standardized client as an educational tool improved my learning experience.

1	2	3	4	5
Strongly Disagree				Strongly Agree

5. I would recommend the continued use of standardized clients as part of the social work curriculum.

1	2	3	4	5
Strongly Disagree				Strongly Agree

6. I would recommend the use of standardized clients to other social work students.

1	2	3	4	5
Strongly Disagree				Strongly Agree

7. Please circle your overall view of the value of standardized clients as a learning experience for social work students.

1	2	3	4	5
Strongly Disagree				Strongly Agree

8. Please provide any suggestions or general comments you have about the use of standardized clients. (Please use reverse side.)

Source: Adapted from Miller (2004).

Pledge of Confidentiality

From class discussion and reading the NASW Code of Ethics, I understand the importance of professional integrity and confidentiality. Because the OSCE is a simulation of professional practice, I understand that all client information I learn about is confidential and not to be communicated to anyone, including classmates.

This pledge has an indefinite time limit.

Student Name (please print): _____

Student Signature: _____

Witness:_____

Date: _____

APPENDIX F
Using Video Recordings of Simulated Practice

Working with families where child maltreatment occurs presents particular challenges for the social worker and is one of the most delicate and anxiety-ridden areas of social work. Social workers who come to the profession hoping to be empathic to their clients must struggle with confronting harmful behavior. They are exposed to vulnerable children who are often in need of protection from their families, as well as to families that are often suffering from deleterious circumstances, past and present trauma, or other adverse conditions.

Training via simulation presents the worker or student of child maltreatment interventions with a unique opportunity to practice his or her diagnostic and treatment skills. Alternatively, the use of video-recorded simulated interviews for teaching in the classroom can also create an important learning experience.

The Haruv Institute in Jerusalem, Israel, which provides research and training in the field of child maltreatment, has been experimenting with the development of learning tools for professionals working in this field. The institute, established in 2007 by the Charles and Lynn Schusterman Family Foundation, is designed to create tailor-made programs for professionals working with this population and to address lacunae in their training agendas. It created a video recording simulating a case of suspected child maltreatment as one method of teaching social workers about the unique issues facing those working with suspected child maltreatment. This appendix describes the objectives, creation, and use of such a recording for use in social work courses.

Learning Objectives

This particular classroom session was designed to help students conceptualize the competencies needed when initiating a first contact with a family where maltreatment is suspected. Our initial focus was on this first intervention because the initial contact is central in setting the stage for collaboration with a family.

Four main treatment issues were identified as critical to the first meeting: presenting the reason for contact (the abuse allegation) and giving a statement of purpose (why the worker has come and what he or she wants to achieve), preliminary assessment, risk assessment and decision making (can the child stay at home, or should he or she be removed immediately?), and agreeing on a contract for ongoing work, if necessary, with the family. In addition, establishing a working relationship with the client and coping with the worker's feelings about the parents and children (countertransference) were also identified as necessary competencies.

Presenting the Reason for Contact

In social work in general, the worker must clarify the client's understanding of the referral, the nature of the agency, and the service that can be provided. In cases of alleged child abuse, this can be a difficult thing to do, and it depends on how much the client already knows about why the social worker is arriving. Although the literature supports providing a clear and honest explanation about the reason for referral, clearly stating the purpose of the contact, and sharing with the client information that is already known about her (Shulman, 2009), the exact wording about how to explain an abuse allegation is one that workers struggle with. This lesson plan stimulates a discussion of how to state such an allegation in a way that will enable continuing dialogue with the family.

Preliminary Assessment

During a psychosocial assessment in any case, the emotional state of all family members, their age-appropriate functioning, their relationships with one another and outside the family, their economic status and position in the community, the ecology of their neighborhood or city, and cultural issues are all important factors to assess. In cases of suspected child abuse, knowledge of child development and of parent–child relationships and an understanding of the psychology of parenthood are paramount. This understanding relates to the assessment process as the social worker tries to determine how dangerous a young mother is to her child and what protective factors exist to help her raise him well.

Risk Assessment and Decision Making

The assessment process leads the social worker to make a decision as to the immediacy of danger to the child and whether his or her immediate removal from the home is necessary or whether other plans can be made. This lesson plan discusses what the social worker asked, saw, and understood about the child's safety at home.

Contract for Ongoing Contact

After the initial contact, the client must be clearly told what will happen next. If the social worker thinks that ongoing contact is necessary, he or she needs to talk about this with the client. This subject is a delicate one given the involuntary nature of the contact: Few clients will want to accept an ongoing relationship that is evaluating and judging their parental ability. How to suggest and promote ongoing contact is therefore an important part of the first meeting and is discussed in this lesson plan.

Importance of Relationship and Countertransference

The professional literature states unequivocally that developing a positive relationship with a social worker achieves positive outcomes for children and families involved with child welfare services (de Boer & Coady, 2007; Lee & Ayon, 2004; Munro, 2011). Research shows that a positive relationship assists with the change process, is associated with improvements in discipline and emotional care, and increases the level of safety afforded the child. During this class, the importance of relationship, and how to create it, is discussed throughout: How can the social worker make the client feel less judged? How does he or she relate to the client's parenting in a way that will promote relationship? Most important, how does the worker deal with countertransference feelings toward a potentially abusive parent to maintain an empathic therapeutic stance?

Creating a Video Recording of a Simulation

We decided to create and video record a scenario of a case of alleged child maltreatment, enacted by a social worker from the Haruv Institute and an actor. We concentrated on physical abuse and designed a case that was not extreme, unclear as to the presence and extent of abuse, and we decided to present a first meeting.

The scenario is of a young, single mother, a new immigrant to Israel, with a 6-month-old baby boy. His child care providers found faint blue marks on his upper arms. Worried that he may have been held too hard, or shaken, and concerned about the mother's apparent depression, they notified social services. The social worker arranged a home visit to find out what was happening with the baby and the mother.

A Young Mother With a Difficult Baby

Background

Anna, age 22, is a single mother of Tommy, age 6 months. She arrived in the country at age 16 from the Ukraine by herself (without her family), in a program for teenagers who wanted to immigrate to Israel, and lived in a boarding school until age 18. She served in the army and spent a year working as a waitress after her army service. At age 19 she met Michael, a young Israeli, and she moved in with him at age 20. Their relationship was tense and stormy, characterized by occasional violence by Michael toward Anna. When she found herself pregnant, he threatened to leave her if she didn't have an abortion. She refused, and he left when she was 5 months pregnant. Anna managed to support herself until late in her pregnancy but had to eventually leave waitressing. She is currently receiving Social Security benefits as a single parent and lives in a tiny apartment with her mother and her son. Michael is not in contact with mother or son.

Anna is the only child of Regina, age 43, also a single mother. Regina decided to immigrate to Israel to help her daughter when Michael left her. She was an engineer in the Ukraine and didn't find compatible work in her new country. She does occasional housekeeping jobs to bring in some income. Regina has very clear ideas about how to raise babies and often criticizes Anna's mothering. Anna, who hasn't lived with her mother since age 16, feels criticized, unsupported, and stifled.

Anna's pregnancy was uneventful. Anna describes herself as being emotionally detached from the growing fetus: "I had to make a living, didn't think about him much." Tommy was born at 38 weeks, and his birth weight was 2.6 kilos. He was hospitalized at age 2 months with respiratory distress and spent a week in hospital. He gained weight slowly and is still a fussy baby who cries a lot, feeds every few hours, and keeps his mother up at night.

Tommy was placed in a daycare center at age 5 months, which the local welfare agency helps to fund. The director of the center describes Tommy as a tense baby who rarely smiles. He comes appropriately dressed and seems to meet most developmental milestones. She contacted Anna's social worker after noticing light bruises on Tommy's upper arms and is worried that he is being shaken or held too tightly. The social worker makes an appointment for a home visit to assess the situation.

The Situation

The social worker arrives in the afternoon, when Anna is home with Tommy. Regina is at work. The living room, which serves as Regina's bedroom, is very small but tidy. Tommy is in an infant rocker. In the middle of the conversation, Tommy begins to cry. He cries hard before Anna picks him up, unwillingly, and holds him with his back to her while she goes to bring him a bottle. The minute he stops eating, she puts him back down in the rocker. There is little reciprocity or joy in their relationship.

Directions to Actor

Anna is a somber and somewhat depressed-looking young woman, dressed in a sweatsuit and sneakers. She is polite but offers no information unless asked. The social worker asks her how things are going with Tommy, and she answers, "He's kind of a hard baby. Cries a lot." When the social worker tells her why she came, she bursts into tears. If the social worker is empathic and can talk about how hard raising the baby is for her, Anna will tell her that she's exhausted, that Tommy doesn't give her any rest, that she has no strength to do anything except sleep when Tommy's in daycare.

If the social worker seems less empathic, she will cry and say, "Everything is fine. I don't know what you're talking about. I'm doing okay. I'm a good mother. I don't know who told you such things about me. He bruises easily."

If the social worker manages to keep the discussion going, Anna will talk about her dream of studying to be a chef, which she can't do now that she is a new mother. She will also add that her mother tries to help, but "she's driving me crazy," and that she's enraged at Michael, who left her and disappeared.

After the scenario was written, a number of points for intervention were identified whereby the social worker acting in the video would relate differently to the situation. One intervention would lead to a poorer result and the other to a better one. Following are the interventions.

Change in intervention I: The first time, the social worker explains in exact words about the report from the daycare center (e.g., "bruises on his arms"). The second time, she explains in a less threatening manner ("The daycare people are worried that you're having a hard time with Tommy").

Change in intervention II: The first time, the social worker gives directions and is less empathic ("takes sides" with the baby: "he's crying, pick him up," "he doesn't have to eat so often," "he needs a lot of love and warmth"). The second time, she is empathic toward the difficulties of the young woman, elicits them, and responds to them.

Change in intervention III: The first time, the social worker does not explicitly check possible danger to the baby (doesn't look at him and check him, doesn't ask). The second time, she gently asks (something like, "Babies who cry a lot can be very annoying to their tired mothers. Have you ever been so angry or upset that you worried what you would do with him?").

Change in intervention IV: The first time, the social worker doesn't check relationships and possible sources of support, especially with grandmother and father. The second time, she asks about these relationships ("Who do you have around who can help you?").

Change in intervention V: The first time, the social worker doesn't summarize what they discussed in the meeting or what she heard is happening with the mother and doesn't suggest a plan (other than making another appointment). The second time, she talks about the young mother's stress and difficulties in relationships, says she's sure that Anna wants to be a good mother, and suggests coming again to make sure that will happen and to think together how to make things better for her.

The video recordings were filmed at the Israel Center for Medical Simulation in the Sheba Medical Center. This center works with the Haruv Institute in creating simulation days for graduates of various professional and training programs. A young female actor played Anna. A doll sat in a baby rocker, and the actor could activate a computer that would make infant crying sounds when appropriate to the moment in the scenario. Approximately 13 parts of a first meeting were video recorded, with the different direction in intervention and the actor/client's ensuing response to each one. Once recorded, a number of segments were chosen for teaching.

Using the Video Recording in the Classroom

This session was given to a small group of social work students, studying for their bachelor's degree (a degree that enables social workers to practice in Israel), who were enrolled in a course on children at risk at the School of Social Work, Hebrew University. The social worker from the Haruv Institute, who wrote the scenario and acted in the recorded interview, was the guest lecturer in that class.

The scenario was distributed to the students (not including the sections "the situation" or "instructions to actor"), who read it. They were asked, "Is this infant at risk?" They enumerated the risk factors they read in the scenario: the marks on the baby's arms, the young age of the mother and the fact that she was grieving the loss of her baby's father, the poverty she was living in, her difficult relationship with her own mother, her appearing not attached to the baby, and the baby's constitutional fussiness.

Next, they were asked, "What does a social worker need to do in the first meeting with such a client?" and they enumerated what they saw as the goals of a first meeting. This gave students the opportunity to conceptualize the competencies needed in the first interview: stating the allegation, assessment, risk assessment and decision making, and creating a beginning contract for ongoing contact.

The video-recorded segments were shown to match the competency to be illustrated. First, a segment was shown where the client reacted badly to the intervention. For instance, on the subject of stating the allegation, the social worker immediately told the client that she was there "because the child care workers saw blue marks on Tommy's arms." The client/actor became upset, and asked the worker, "Is that why you came? You think I'm abusing my child? You want to take him from me?" In the second scenario, the social worker said that the child care workers were worried about her and about the baby and noticed that they are both tired and unhappy. The social worker also stated that her job is "to make sure that families are getting along well and that parents and children are okay." The client was able to describe her difficulties much more frankly with this intervention. The ensuing discussion with the students included ethical questions (Is it ethical to not explicitly state the reason for intervention?) and questions about pacing and relationship (When does one bring up the explicit allegation in such a case and with what wording? How does one convey empathy while speaking to a mother about her potentially harming her child?).

The second two recorded segments showed the baby crying while the mother ignored his cries. In the first segment, the social worker instructed the mother to pick him up, saying things such as "A baby needs his mother's arms. You know that babies need warmth and closeness, don't you?" In the second segment, the worker spoke to the baby, saying, "You really want your mother," and pointed out how the child responds differentially to her (the social worker says, "I spoke to him and he looked at me as if to say, 'Who are you?' With you, it's different."). She also said that she saw how difficult it was for the mother to pick him up when she's so tired.

These vignettes were used both for assessment purposes and to examine ways of intervening with a mother who feels emotionally distanced from her child. The importance and ways of making a rough assessment about infant attachment was discussed with the students. The mother's ability to make use of the intervention to become closer to her child was also seen as a strength.

The next two competencies, risk assessment and decision making, and making a beginning contract for ongoing intervention were illustrated and discussed in the same way. The video-recorded segments of the simulation generated the discussion. In the area of decision making, the question about whether the child could be safely left alone with the mother was addressed as a critical component of a first contact. In the area of contract, working with involuntary clients and presenting honest yet palatable reasons for continuing contact were discussed.

Student and Staff Reactions to the Session

One of the most noticeable reactions of students to the session was that they were entranced and moved by the video recordings. They stated that the videos felt very real and that they lost track of the fact that it wasn't a real meeting. They spoke of their frustration at not being able to see real social work in action, and use of the videos helped them imagine real situations. In addition, they were very preoccupied with the question of how one uses relationship to further such work. They understood from the video recording that the more relationship-building interventions the social worker made, the more the client shared her world and responded to her child. On the other hand, the fact that this is not an extreme case and that sometimes clients are much more hostile and children are much more at risk made them wonder how to balance empathy with their worry over potential harm to the child.

Summary

The use of video-recorded simulated interviews in teaching about intervention in child maltreatment cases is a useful and evocative way of adapting simulation to the classroom when actual simulation is not available. The realistic nature of the videos, which allows students to imagine how they would react in the situation, and a clear lesson plan that conceptualizes the competencies required provide students with a clear picture of what to keep in mind and how to intervene in such cases. Furthermore, defining the goals of the first meeting and showing the stages of such a meeting were considered very important to students.

Source: Developed by Paula David, director, Department of Learning Programs, Haruv Institute, Jerusalem, Israel.

INDEX

ABOUT THE AUTHORS

MARION BOGO is professor at the Factor-Inwentash Faculty of Social Work, University of Toronto. Her research focuses on field education and the development and testing of innovative approaches to assessment of student competence. She has published widely on social work education and practice and consulted to schools of social work in North America, Asia, and Europe. In 2013 she was awarded the Significant Lifetime Achievement in Social Work Education Award from the Council of Social Work Education in recognition of her contributions to social work education and to improving assessment of professional competence. In 2014 she was appointed as an Officer of the Order of Canada for her achievements in the field of social work as a scholar and teacher, and for advancing the practice in Canada and abroad.

MARY RAWLINGS is professor at Azusa Pacific University, chair of the Department of Social Work, and director of the MSW program. Her teaching and research interests are in competency based education and the development and testing of the use of simulation in training and assessment of student practice skill. She is interested in experiential learning models, such as service-learning, that can enhance student educational outcomes. She currently conducts research on the development of OSCE exams for social work. She is a licensed clinical social worker with more than 10 years of practice experience. Her practice interests are in women's issues and chronic and persistent mental illness.

ELLEN KATZ is lecturer and director of Continuing Education at the Factor-Inwentash Faculty of Social Work, University of Toronto and is an academic clinical educator at the Hincks-Dellcrest Centre in Toronto. Her research and clinical interests focus on simulation, the development of competence in students and clinicians, and on mindfulness and family therapy. She has more than 20 years of clinical practice working with individuals, couples, families, and groups in hospitals and children's mental health settings. She has a particular interest and advanced training in family therapy.

CARMEN LOGIE is assistant professor at the Factor-Inwentash Faculty of Social Work, University of Toronto. Her research focuses on health equity, with particular attention to the associations between intersectional forms of stigma and health outcomes, and implications for social work and public health practice. She has published on social and structural drivers of health, intersectional stigma, LGBTQ health and affirmative practice recommendations, and community-based interventions.